The Great Book of Wealth Creation

Guide for Building Wealth through the Journey of Life.

Mukesh Jangid

ISBN 978-93-5458-639-2
© Mukesh Jangid 2021
Published in India 2021 by Pencil

A brand of

One Point Six Technologies Pvt. Ltd.
123, Building J2, Shram Seva Premises,
Wadala Truck Terminal, Wadala (E)
Mumbai 400037, Maharashtra, INDIA
E connect@thepencilapp.com
W www.thepencilapp.com

Author biography

Mukesh Jangid

Founder with a demonstrated history of working in the consulting industry and the Share Market.

Skilled in Data Analysis, Entrepreneurship, and Customer Analysis.

Mukesh Jangid is Business savvy - He design evaluates and justifies strategic solutions from a thorough understanding of the business which could benefit your business.

Choosing him can give you the following benefits to your business:-

- Business Growth

- Boost Revenues

- Reduce Costs

- Gain Productivity

- Make data-driven decisions.

He helps people and their businesses *GROW.*

CONTENTS

Preface

Growing Wealth. Wise Investment. Good Returns. Big Profits. Good Income. Financial Freedom.

These words are so heavy and amazing, right? Everyone is trying to achieve these in safe and simple ways. But what's safe and simple?

For the whole world, Covid-19 was a shock and no one imagined or thought that one day the whole world can face such a big problem. Now we can see many people losing their jobs, problems of unemployment getting increased, businesses getting closed, about 12% of startups got closed, 70% of startups facing big problems, GDP of the countries has fallen badly and it all hurts to financial health.

So what's safe then? How to grow wealth, how to make good profits, how to invest wisely?

I would say that one must invest in **Opportunities**. We have gone through many crises in the past, like the

1929 market crash, the 2008 recession, and every time we came out shining. Rightly said, "This time shall pass!" But, we need to be prepared and need to maintain our strong financial health by grabbing those available opportunities around us.

We need to focus on getting skills that will help us in situations like Covid-19 which was not in our control and which impacted badly on our financial health. People with good skills made good money via Trading and Investing (when many businesses were closed and people had lockdown situations, they worked from home, Share Market was open and people made good money from trading) or starting business of Sanitizers or masks or such startups which solved problems at the right time.

We are talking about opportunities and investments, right? From March 2020, Nifty made a low of around 7600, and in September 2021, it was trading at 17400. Huge returns in less than 2 years. Dozens of stocks gave more than 200% returns in this Covid-19 pandemic. At the time, not only Share Market but we have seen people starting a new business with some good ideas which solved problems, the business of masks, sanitizer sells, work from home services like online courses, etc. and those people got good benefitted. These are all good opportunities. If we can't start a business then at least we can invest in a business we understand and we can get good returns. Isn't it?

Skills and talents will help us in all situations and people with good skills will survive in the fast-changing world. Those skills and good knowledge will help us to find good opportunities. When it comes to financial health we need to set up ourselves well with good management and good plans.

Hence, I tried to put some good articles on investment, business ideas, financial planning, and importantly a mini-course of trading that will help you.

According to my experience, I can say that the Share Market provides us bundles of Opportunities every single day. We need to improve our skills and grab those good moneymaking opportunities just like an Eagle. In this book, I will share my experience and knowledge so you too can grab those moneymaking opportunities by learning and practicing my ideas and methods on the Share Market and will be sharing some good fruitful, and amazing articles on starting a new business or making a good financial plan which will help you the most.

Acknowledgements

I am blessed to have two amazing women in my life, who supported me and taught me some great valuable things.

My mother was a great fighter and she fought hard with Cancer but unfortunately, I lost her in April 2019.

She fought with a smile till her last breath and taught me the lesson of Never Giving Up. I do remember her smile and will cherish that for life long.

Again, my wife supported me well in all moments and so I would dedicate this book to both of them, as they made me what I am today.

Love to my daughter **Kashish.**

Introduction

I will share my personal experience of investments and you will be able to relate and help you get some ideas and plans to invest your time and money wisely.

To be frank and direct,

When I was young, I thought of getting a job in the IT industry and so did my Engineering in Information Technology. So my father invested his money to get my degree so I can get a good job in IT companies. But later on, ***I understood that Academic Education will land me in a 9-5 job and Financial Education will bring me out of that and I can get my dreams and financial freedom in a better way.***

I always had a creative and brainstorming mind playing with some thoughts with ongoing situations and so I felt to quit my job and I started a Venture. While running the business I learned about various aspects of business and got good practical knowledge of Market, Sales, Accounts, and a lot of things that work together and result in good returns for the company/business.

In doing so I got to know about the Share Market and I invested my money to get knowledge of the Share Market. All this was unintentional and unplanned and I walked in my life where my destiny was taking me. After getting into the Share Market and trading for a few years I got the best practical knowledge of trading and I learned the Art of Trading and Art of Wise Investments in terms of time and money.

Now with all these good experiences and wise investments, today **I have a good grasp of the markets and I focus on getting more out of everything as generating good profits from trading, investing, and consulting new startups and businesses.**

This concludes that the best investment I made was in me which helped me to get good skills and talent. I improved myself and tried to get better every single day. Today I am much satisfied with the result of my investment returns.

Investing in yourself is the best thing you can do. If you have got talents, no one can take them from you.

- Warren Buffett

Usain Bolt won 8 gold medals in the 3 Olympics, and he only ran for less than 115 seconds on the track, earning $119M dollars. That's an economy of effort.

But for those 2 minutes, he trained for 20 years. That's an investment. Think long-term. Patience pays. Trust on skills.

Skills, talent and good management do wonders J

In 2014, Todd Kunsman, founder of the personal finance blog Invested Wallet, was $29,000 in debt and working a job that paid less than $36,000 per year. Kunsman decided to take the reins of his finances and improve his situation, educating himself on topics like investing and money at large.

"I decided to dedicate an hour or two each week to learning about personal finance," he tells Grow (media company).

"I would highlight key sections and take notes on my phone to remember points that stood out to me."

Today, he has not only paid his debt but also saved more than $100,000.

But that's just past things right? We can't change the past right? But what we can do is think of the future and prepare ourselves for a better future.

Let's divine the future and as the future is going to be a technical revolution and will see huge changes around.

Let's see...

We have seen advertisements on television, drones carrying pizza, and delivering us. Alexa providing us services of turning lights ON and OFF, playing songs, booking our tickets, providing us news, and answering our questions within a few minutes or seconds. It's just the start of Artificial Intelligence which is present in our homes, in our cars and I can say soon will see it everywhere. The next 10-15 years will see massive changes and we should prepare ourselves well.

Companies are working and putting a lot of money into Artificial Intelligence. So why do you need this knowledge?

It's just because it will impact on jobs and careers people are having now. If people don't improve their skills and change according to time, then surely it will impact severely on the jobs as robotics are now invented and trained to take those people jobs and do things faster.

We are making achievements in technology and drones is just a smaller of what we are looking at. Drones are already there and soon will see many more flying in the sky and providing more services like carrying a critical piece of medical equipment to a hospital to make sure it doesn't get stuck in traffic. Or helping to keep an eye on an important caravan so people know on the ground if there is a problem? There are so many ways drones can affect our world. I can see that drones will be part of our integral life. We have cars that are safer than in the last decade, and we are even building fully electric cars and self-driving cars and so drivers will lose their jobs and drown delivery systems so the delivery person will lose their jobs.

It's a technological revolution, which means human jobs will be replaced by machines (robots). Already we have seen a great change in the past 10-15 years and looking at the speed how things are changing, it's for sure that a few years later will see major changes in technology and all sectors around the world. The knowledge or skills or education which a doctor needs is it takes around 10-15 years to become a good surgeon, whereas robots will need less than 10 minutes. Because it's an internet world and one can connect faster to anyone to take knowledge from experienced people quickly. Isn't it great? Isn't it a threat for everyone who's unskilled or thinking of not learning or adapting to new things? So are we prepared for that?

We need to focus on the creative talent we have and we need to improve that. So that talent will help us to find new opportunities and take the advantage of that idea and opportunity. As some wealthy people say "Good Idea is real Wealth".

Ideas where we can start from zero just by good great knowledge. So invest your time wisely to learn things and which will help you to level up to the next level according to need and changes.

So at times, I can say that having any good skill or talent is very much important when we are done with Covid-19 lessons. The economy, job situations, growing population, many factors provides us a hint to make ourselves on alert and learn things and invest our time wisely so we can get our financial freedom in a better way.

Time is changing so fast and hence we need to improve ourselves in a better way and build a mindset to grab some good opportunities by having good great knowledge and skills. As better we are and so better will be our wealth.

Let's start...

1. Making Opportunities Count

Opportunity. It's not a word, but I can say it's an event that will make us feel happy, enlighten us, and change us to be better and better.

What is Opportunity?

An opportunity is anything that provides you with a chance to change your circumstances for the better.

Wouldn't you like to experience more, earn more money, or simply be happier? We all want that but aren't necessarily ready to take the risks by ourselves. Sometimes we haven't even thought about doing something until someone or something prompts us.

To achieve anything in life, we need to take a chance. The beauty of taking chances is that anything can happen. You might fall, get hurt, or be embarrassed, but what if you could experience something that is completely mind-blowing and changes your life forever.

Do you think that we would have seen any entrepreneur succeed without taking a chance? All those great entrepreneurs took a step to change their circumstances. But wait, it's not about taking any big chance or big risk. Sometimes a small risk or chance can make a difference for an individual. Let's take a step and shine. Spark your mind towards getting much better financial health.

Business opportunities are like buses, there's always another one coming.

- Richard Branson

One can make good wealth, get good returns, get good profits if he finds that good opportunity, and takes a chance to make it count. We have seen many entrepreneurs who have taken a chance on an idea and invented something which changed their lives and they live their dream life, fulfilling their life's purpose, enjoying financial freedom. But those people aren't just got things by luck or chance. Opportunities are present all around you as well; you just need to learn how to identify and step into them. If we can make good use of those business or money-making opportunities then success will hold and hug us for sure!

I will share the secrets of how one can make good wealth (money) in the long run in the Share Market or from any business idea. Use proper plan and always make yearly, quarterly and monthly plans if you're trading or investing in the share market or starting a business (do make proper analysis from time to time). E.g. make a 15-20 years plan, then break that into 5 years, again in 1 year, again in 6 months, again in 1 month, so you will get to know what you want to do actually in this month itself.

1. **Clarify Goal**- Imagine the goal so deeply that your physiology will respond to an image in your head as if it were reality. (Getting 3 Crores in the next 10 years can be a goal).

2. **Take Consistent Action**and Keep an action tracker and always track your performance and actions if you're taking your daily steps in the right way. (Learning the art of trading and starting with small capital can be the first step.)

3. **Always keep a backup plan**. Good brainstorming will help you get good plans as things might not work always as we plan and so we need another plan as we can't change goals but can have other better plans. (Different trading methods styles will need different plans and strategies).

4. **Data Analysis**is the greatest tool to improve and get the right path and it helps us to make the right decisions.

5. If you are a trader then I will advise you to take your monthly profits and increase trading capital every after 6 months only if your strategies are working and you have gained enough experience and confidence.

6. Keep compounding your profit money in as many 2-3 investment things. As compounding does the actual magic to grow your wealth enormously.

7. **Plan. Execute. Repeat**(unless you're done to achieve 10 Crore).

I think people should stop thinking about unemployment and should focus on the opportunities they are getting. If we have a working brain and a seeing eye, there are thousands of things to be done right around us.

We need skills, wise time utilization, and well executions.

In a conversation with an Uber driver, he told me that he's working in an IT MNC company and still works with Uber to learn new things and earn extra income and he said he makes good returns as he understands the Uber algorithm better than other drivers. Rightly said, no work is small when dreams matter most!

Remember the question from one of the classic *Akbar-Birbal stories - What is the thing that travels the fastest in the world?*

Back in the days of Mughal Emperors, travel was typically by bullock carts, horseback, etc. While Birbal did not come up with any forward-looking vision of the Hyperloop or an airplane or bullet train, he responded by saying, "The fastest thing in the world is not the horse or wind or light or sound, but it is the mind which can take you from your throne in this court to anywhere else in this world in the next second."

So give your mind the work that will yield some good returns. Your subconscious mind is the gatekeeper of your comfort zone. So permit yourself to be happy and successful.

When you pay attention to something, you are buying an experience. It's an investment, so spend it carefully and on the wise things. Treat your time with as much care as your finances. It's equally valuable. I am confident that the book journey will provide you some good great ideas and valuable things and reading it with focus and with little brainstorming will do some great magic.

So let's begin the journey...

2. Turning 3 lakhs to 1 Crore

Yes, it's possible and we have seen many great leaders, the entrepreneurs turned their fortunes and done great things. Good skills, a proper plan, and the right execution can make fortunes.

I will share an example so could get an idea of making 3 lakhs to 1 Crore.

A person starts trading after learning and getting good great knowledge. He starts with an initial 3 lakhs capital.

He gets a decent profit of 2% a month. 2% of 3 lakhs means Rs.6000.

So is that possible to make Rs.6000 from 3 lakhs? Yes, it's very much possible. How? I will share an example,

Bank Nifty moves around 400-1000 points every day. If we can make 65 points with 100 quantities then we are making an Rs.6500 profit.

Suppose Bank Nifty options premium is 100 Rs. (Refer Topic 2) So our investment in buying that option is $100*100 = 10000$Rs. Now when options move to 165 we are making 65 points i.e. Profit of Rs.6500. And if we deduct brokerage and taxes, then roughly still we make Rs.6000.

Also, in Bank Nifty Futures if we get 65 points with 100 quantities then we can make Rs.6500.

One thing is sure that it's not that we can get fixed returns or profits, but we are talking about monthly returns, not daily returns. So month-wise 2% looks possible if we have good knowledge and skills of trading.

Now when we keep doing this same and earn 2% monthly and if we keep compounding then we are making 1 Crore in 15 years and that's true as Maths doesn't lie. Have a look at the table below.

Year	Year Interest	Total Interest	Balance
1	80472	80472	380472
2	102058	182531	482531
3	129435	311966	611966
4	164154	476121	776121
5	208188	684309	984309
6	264032	948342	1248342
7	334857	1283199	1583199
8	424680	1707879	2007879
9	538597	2246477	2546477
10	683071	2929548	3229548
11	866300	3795848	4095848
12	1098677	4894526	5194526
13	1393389	6287915	6587915
14	1767154	8055070	8355070
15	2241179	10296249	10596249

Fig. 1. Compound Interest is calculated monthly with 2% returns.

With Rs.3,00,000 and getting monthly 2% returns on our capital and when we compound it monthly then we are making a profit of Rs.80472.54 in the first year and Rs.102058.64 in the second year and so on. In 15 years with the same compounding of 2% returns a month we are achieving our target of 1 Crore. Surely there can be ups and downs, will be having drawdowns to capital as well, but when we are having drawdowns will be putting experience to our bucket and that will help us to recover, again if we are disciplined and don't repeat the same mistake again which caused us a drawdown, we can bounce back with better results, all important is to keep track of our targets and achieve smaller milestones. It looks easy, but it's not that easy and not impossible also :)

Also, if we find a business that can double our capital every 3 years and if we start with 10 lakhs and continue the same for the next 30 years then we are making 100 Crores. India is a growing country and the population and the young generation helps India gain its wealth and grow GDP. India is working day and night and we have good opportunities around us. If you ask a wise man what's the right time to invest our money then he will say that the best day was yesterday but the next best day is today :) We need to focus on the next 25-30 years and should invest wisely. Today's small monthly investment of thousands can turn to Crores in 20-30 years.

When you start something and keep doing and improving things, then you will get much more as you have got that extra edge of being experienced. So start now, learn things, keep practicing, keep evolving, keep earning, and keep gaining good experience to make a better future!

Investment Gifts

On special occasions, we do give gifts and get return gifts from friends and relatives. I can say that we can start giving the Company shares as gifts, as that can be very useful to them in the future.

On daughter's day, a dad gifted 500 shares of the company worth 10,000 Rupees to her daughter when she was five years old. After 20 years, those 500 shares turned to 1500 (by getting a bonus), and the share price turned to 2000. That means Rs.10,000 turned to 30 lakhs. Isn't it great?

3. Mistakes to avoid in Financial Life

I will share one example, and you will be able to relate financial mistakes which people often make in their financial life.

Mr. Ashish is 30 years old and currently earning Rs1.5 lakhs/month. He started his career at the age of 24 with a salary of Rs. 50,000/month. In the last ten years, he took many decisions on the financial front. So let us see his financial journey of the last ten years.

Mr. Ashish joined a big company with a handsome salary of Rs.50,000 in 2009. Just like many of us he had many temptations like buying a new iPhone, purchasing a new car, and many others.

So within two months of joining he purchased a new iPhone and after a year, he decided to purchase a car of Rs 5 Lakhs on Loan. Obviously status in society matters for millennials like us.

Further enjoying every weekend by watching movies and dining out was on his priority list. He had barely any money to save. So his first financial decision of earning life was to purchase a gadget, purchase a car on loan, and enjoying weekends. ***Loans and too many expenses are***

the FIRST MISTAKE of his financial life.Hence, rather than making money from the money, he is killing money.

2 years into the job, but our dear friend Ashish hadn't saved anything yet. But he got the enlightenment one day that he has to save some money. So he decided that whatever will be left at the end of the month he will transfer it into another account for saving. ***The SECOND MISTAKE of his financial life has first been spent and then save.***It should be the other way around by saving at least some amount first and then spending whatever is left.

Nonetheless, at least he was saving now some amount. The saved money was kept on saving account at a meager interest rate of 4% and after two years of saving he moved that amount into FD at an interest rate of 8% and purchased some physical gold for an investment purpose. ***The THIRD MISTAKE of his financial life is investing all of his money in debt products and hence rarely able to defeat inflation.***(Post-tax returns in FD are merely 6. 5–7%. Also, while purchasing physical gold you are giving making charges and while selling the gold jewels deduct money based on the purity of gold and hence low returns). Hence, in this case too despite making wealth for his future, he is losing the purchasing power of his money. Also, taxes paid will dilute the income, and we end up getting lesser returns, and so we need to have a proper plan for everything we are doing in terms of financial works.

He is 29 now and has completed 5 years in his job. Also, he has achieved another milestone in his personal life; he is now married to Ms. Radhika. His wife is working too, and now he has a dual salary coming to his home.

Both of them now decided that they shall purchase a home. Their parents and their relatives had a huge influence on this decision of theirs. They made a down payment of 25 Lakhs (the amount they saved in form of FD's and some borrowing from parents) and took a home loan of 60 Lakhs. ***The FOURTH MISTAKE of his financial life is to purchase real estate by spending all his liquid money.***They had spent all the amount they saved to date. Now in case of some emergency (maybe job loss or any other major expense as we have seen in the Covid-19 period), they don't have an emergency fund to fall upon. Real estate is highly illiquid and also they can't sell 200 Sqft out of 1200 Sqft flat as they have to meet some emergency.

Mr. Ashish is 33 years old and is blessed with a baby girl. He and his family are extremely happy. His expenses have further increased with the addition of a new family member. He also has a home loan going on and also his lifestyle expenses are also increasing.

Coming in 2019 when he is 34 years old his financial life looks like this - Tax saving through PPF and endowment plans, Home loan EMI's, CAR LOAN EMI (Upgraded to SEDAN), and monthly expenditure. He and his wife are saving money in FD's and some money in saving accounts. ***FIFTH MISTAKE of his financial life; unaware of his financial goals.***He has certain financial goals ahead; Education of his daughter, the Marriage of his daughter, and his retirement to name a few. Rather than quantifying his goals as per the timeline and accordingly choosing financial products he is only investing money in an endowment plan, PPF, and FD's.

***SIXTH MISTAKE** of his financial life; not linking financial goals with the apt financial products.*

You have just gone through his 10-year journey and have seen seven personal finance mistakes he has done. If you find yourself making some or many of these mistakes, which I am sure you are, personal finance knowledge is extremely important for you. I feel there is a certain age in life where good hard work and saving pays off really well for around 15-20 years. After that, it's difficult to find pace and energy.

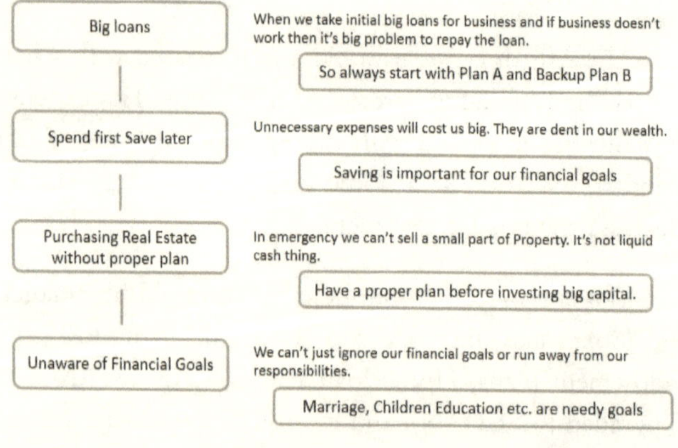

Fig. 2. Mistakes to avoid in Financial Planning (Flowchart).

So what's a good plan? How to make a good financial plan?

Let's move further to get the plan.

4. Good Plan

"Our goals can only be reached through a vehicle of a plan, in which we must fervently believe, and upon which we must vigorously act. There is no other route to success." — **Pablo Picasso**

Rightly said as planning is considered as the first step towards reaching one's goal. According to my experience, I will share a Good Plan which will help you to achieve your financial freedom in a better way. Here's the plan:

1.No debt to start anything with.

2.Get a job. Divide the income into 5 ways:

1. Living expenses.

2. Life goals, savings. (Marriage, car, education, etc.)

3. Emergency savings.

4. Investment options. (Let it compound)

5. Start an online home business. Divide the income 5 ways:

1. Living expenses.

2. Life goals, savings. (Marriage, car, education, etc.)

3. Emergency savings.

4. Investment options. (Let it compound)

5. Start an online business. Divide the income 5 ways: (well, you get the idea)

3.Quit the job once you have 3–5 stable online businesses. Then:

1. Sell one business and buy real estate and rent it.

2. Create a new online business and wait for it to mature. Then:

1. Sell one business and buy real estate and rent it.

2. Create a new online business and wait for it to mature. Then: (you get the idea, repeat)

4.Now you have 3–5 real estate. Use their rent to buy more real estate.

5.Now you have

1. Financial investment portfolio compounding.

2. Real estate rents.

3. Online business income.

6.Sell all remaining online businesses and put the money in the financial investment portfolio and let it compound.

7.If you have 5–10 real estates you can retire on the rents. Let the financial portfolio compound.

8.When the financial portfolio matures take half the profits every year and add it on top of the rent money and live like a king.

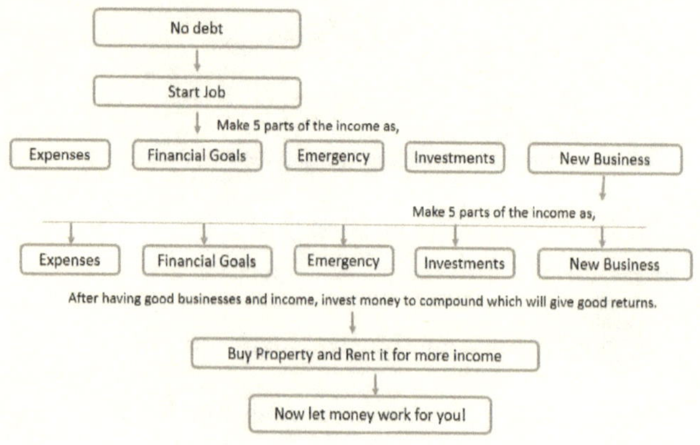

Fig. 3. Planning flowchart.

This process can take anywhere from 5–15 years to finish. The key is to

1. Stay out of debt so you can try as many times as possible with online businesses, no matter how many times you fail you can try again next month, unlike with debt. After the next 5 years.

2. Create as many sources of income as possible, not just to increase the revenues, but to dilute the risk of losing one source of income or another.

3. When in doubt... Compound. The whole point is reinvesting most of your revenue and spending less than one source of income.

But, everyone doesn't want to jump into business or can't start a business. That's right. What we can do is, we can invest in the business and get returns. Investment in companies is a good option and so will share an article by which we can invest and manage our equity portfolio for getting good returns.

Here we go…

5. Managing Portfolio

A good well-constructed equity portfolio is important to wealth creation. But we need to understand that the Share Market is not a place for gambling, and we shouldn't choose any risky or hero zero stocks just by seeing the very low price of the company share. People often make these mistakes and choose stocks on friends', relative's advice and hold the shares on hopes and don't use any plan, analysis, or skills to manage the portfolio and loses capital instead of gaining.

So what's the best way to manage and get a good portfolio?

According to my experience, I will share some steps and methods by which you can hold and manage a good equity portfolio.

1. **Goals:**We need to have a proper plan and set good realistic goals before we jump into making an equity portfolio. We should know the reason we are investing in it. So we can get the answers to where to invest when to invest and how much to invest. After getting a good plan of goals we can set a period and choose stocks accordingly.

2. **Analyze the Market Trend:**A good trendy market gives us good returns and we need to analyze the Bull trend of the Market to invest at right time.

3. **Investing in Business:**We need to invest in a business that we understand well. While making a watch list of stocks we need to analyze the companies on basis of their Management, Business model, and Valuations of the company. We should focus on quality not quantities to get good decent returns. Savings Interest Rates which we get in Financial Institutions (Banks Savings, FD's RD's) of 3-4% is not going to help us to grow our wealth, as the inflation rate is around 5-6% and that makes people invest in stocks and get good decent returns.

4. **Sectors:**According to our goals we need to identify well-performing sectors. Sectors which are expected to do well in the next 10-15 years and we need to choose 2-3 sectors and invest in those 2-3 sectors rather than putting all in one sector which is quite a risky bet.

5. **Analyze Stocks**: After selecting good 2-3 sectors, we need to select 3-4 stocks in each sector to invest in. We should have 8-10 stocks according to our personality and shouldn't jump to invest in more stocks like 30-50 stocks as that will be hard for us to observe and analyze them regularly. Those 8-10 stocks we need to observe and have their quarterly reports and we should manage their

positions according to the current analysis as no one is right every time we buy the stock. We need to analyze stocks on a fundamental and technical basis to identify the best time of investment.

6. **Price:**Rightly said that "Price is God" when it comes to investments. We should see if our all criteria are met. A good price can give us good returns. Just because the share price is low doesn't mean it's good. People do make mistakes and think that it's already fallen and how much more it can fall and jumps to invest by seeing the low price. We need to analyze the best time and share price of the company.

7. **Position Sizing:**Before making large initial positions it's better to start with 40-50% and buy more when we see the strength in the stock as per our goal requirements.

8. **In-between Checks:**There is always a risk, which is not in our control. The market often reacts to Government policies, or we can have the Covid-19 crisis where the Market can give good corrections. And at those correction times, we can't hold stocks for a longer time and should cut our losses at right time and invest again when the stock starts its bull run again. We can't catch exact low or highs to buy or sell so we need to enter and exit as per our risk aptitudes.

9. **Winning Stocks:**One or two stocks can be performing superbly well and so our goal is to allocate more capital to our best stocks. Those

winning stocks will be vital for our wealth creations.

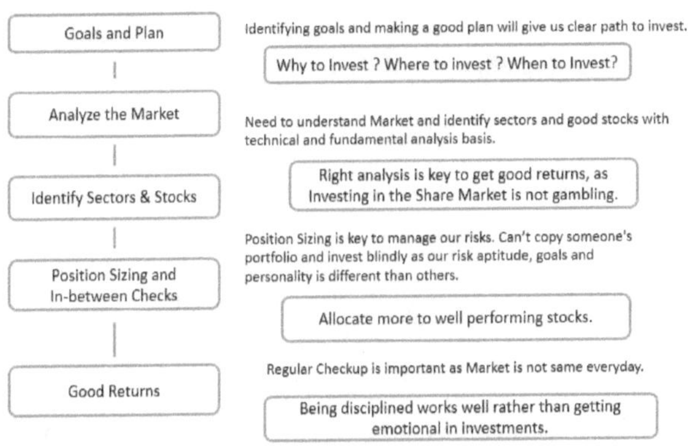

Fig. 4. Steps for Managing Equity Portfolio

Wait. Looks like you need an example of how patience works and how one can get benefitted by investing and getting a bonus, dividends from the company. Let's see an example of a person who invested Rs.10,000 and got 500 Crores from it.

Wealth Creation Journey

Wealthy is a great word, and everyone feels happy and aims to be one. But there are so many definitions of wealth, and it means different to everyone.

For some people having more money means being wealthy, and more valuable material possessions or resources means being wealthy. Some people think that having a good Idea means being wealthy. Some people think that Health is Wealth. Some people think having a good business means being wealthy. For some people having a luxurious life means being wealthy.

Again, being rich and being wealthy is different. Like,

Your brother-in-law is Rich, and Mukesh Ambani is wealthy.

Wealthy people save and invest wisely.

We use the money to save time. We order food online so we can make our time and effort in cooking. And in this technological world, it's very important to save and invest our time wisely. Time is the great equalizer, rich or poor, we all have the same 24 hours in a day.

The journey to wealth creation is not only about wealth creation through wise and disciplined investments, but it's also about preserving and multiplying wealth.

Wealth Creation is not arriving at one destination. It is a continuous process of moving ahead and achieving various milestones in life and we need to level up ourselves in this technological revolution.

We have seen many wealthy people turned zero, and many people turned from zero to wealthy. So important is to know the process and path to Become Wealthy. Great business, great ideas, good skills, and good knowledge are the weapons by which we can win the war. So let's start the journey.

Investment of 10,000 grows to 500 Crore

A person invested Rs. 10,000 in 1980 in a company and bought 100 Shares at 100 Rs each and invested after understanding the business of the Company and thought as his running the company and will hold shares for a longer time.

The initial investment was Rs. 10,000.

In 1981, the company declared a 1:1 bonus. He now had 200 shares.

In 1985, the company declared a 1:1 bonus. He, therefore, had 400 shares.

In 1986, the company split the share to Rs.10. He thus had 4000 shares.

In 1987, the company declared a 1:1 bonus. He hence had 8000 shares.

In 1989, the company announced a 1:1 bonus. Now he had 16,000 shares.

In 1992, the company declared a 1:1 bonus. By now he had 32,000 shares.

In 1995, the company declared a 1:1 bonus. He then had 64,000 shares.

In 1997, the company declared a 2:1 bonus. He now held 1,92,000 shares.

In 1999, the company split the share to Rs.2. He now had 9,60,000 shares.

In 2004, the company declared a 2:1 bonus. He thus had 28,80,000 shares.

In 2005, the company declared a 1:1 bonus. He came to have 57,60,000 shares.

In 2010, the company declared a 2:3 bonus. He now had 96,00,000 shares.

If the current market price is Rs.500 per share. The shares are valued at Rs.480 crores.

Over the past 33 years, the company regularly paid out dividends and increased them almost every year. Cumulatively he received Rs.118 crores as dividends over the past 33 years. Thus by investing Rs.10,000, a person gained Rs.598 crores.

This is how patience wins and generates more wealth.

Wipro, Infosys, and many more Companies in which people invested earlier have turned those thousands to Crores.

Disclaimer: The story is only for illustration purposes. This report is not intended to be taken as financial advice. This report is only for your personal use and is not intended for any business purpose. However, I do not guarantee the accuracy, adequacy, or completeness of any information and am not responsible for any errors or omissions or the results obtained from the use of such information. Only shared for educational purposes.

But wait. You want to start a business right? But don't have time and already having a job running then how to start a business. What's the plan?

Let's see...

6. Small Business Ideas

How to Start Your Own Business? How to make small business ideas?

What can I do to create another source of income?

As Jack Ma, Founder of Alibaba put it:

What you do after work determines your future?

Let's say you come back from work at 5 pm, and you go to sleep at midnight. That gives you 7 hours in between. The first question you should ask is:

How do you currently spend these 7 hours?

Before I get into what can be done, let's try and understand a very important concept:

Time value of money.

Let's take an example of two friends Karan and Arjun

Karan works in a 9–5 job, Monday to Friday, and earns Rs 50,000 per month in hand.

Total number of hours worked per day = 8

Total number of hours worked per week = 40

Total number of hours worked per month (assuming 22 days) = 176

Salary per month = Rs 50000

Salary per hour = Rs 284

Now, let's say if Karan works overtime of about 20 hours in a month, then his total working hours in the month would be:

196 hours (176+20)

According to this shouldn't he be paid a salary of Rs 55664 (284* 196) per month?

But as most of us can relate to, Karan would get a fixed salary every month regardless of hours put in. At best he would get an appreciation certificate for all his hard work in the annual leadership summit at the company.

Arjun, on the other hand, is a freelance photographer. He blogs, makes videos, does regular shoots, and often lands up some big assignments.

Now obviously Arjun does not have any fixed days or hours of working nor does any weekend off. He is generally anywhere between 20 to 60 hours a week.

Here is the important thing though. If let's say Arjun out of all his activities, earns on an average Rs 500 per hour, he can earn anywhere close to Rs 10000 to Rs 30000 in a week, and Rs 40000 to Rs 120000 in a month.

Unlike Karan, he can increase/decrease his efforts every day because he knows that he will only get paid for the time he puts in. In this case, if he decided to go overboard and out 100 hours in a month, his monthly take-home could easily go up to Rs 200,000.

Now by sharing the two examples above, I don't mean to suggest that you leave your 9–5 jobs and just start freelancing!

The message I want to convey is:

- **Make every hour count at work:**Even if you are in a 9–5 job, make sure you are not doing what 100 of your other team members are doing. Be an entrepreneur within your team and try out different ideas/ways to do a particular thing. Maybe you won't get paid more, but you will go to work every day motivated and obviously when you do something different, you are bound to be noticed, opening doors to opportunities.

- **Use after work hours productively:**There is a friend of mine who is an Economics graduate but is interested in entrepreneurship. During the day he does his job of teaching college graduates, but after work, he does entrepreneurship courses and learned a lot of knowledge on how to start a company. Eventually, he found his own company and sold it, and reaped the rewards.

- **Be a value adder:**The more value you can add to somebody, the more money you can make. And to make more value, you have to be good at your skills. Surely you must be good at something apart from your 9–5 job?

As in the Covid-19 period, we have seen many people either losing their job or getting half salaries even after working the full hours from home. Also, people with good trading skills made money from trading, and people with good business skills started a new business.

Do you love cooking?

Be good at it and start a simple WordPress blog or your own YouTube channel. Monetize that once you have a good number of followers.

Do you love dancing?

Be good at it and rent out a small space and start your dancing class. Or create your own YouTube channel and use Instagram marketing to increase your number of followers to monetize your YouTube channel.

So make effective and productive use of your time, and it can give you wonderful returns.

I have seen a small family having a small samosa shop. And just for curiosity, I asked about how much it cost and how many sales they make in a month. They said they are providing samosa at Rs 15. Do you know how much % profit they get? It's around 60-70%. Or Even if we take minimum 5Rs per samosa and on average, they sell monthly 15000 samosas and with that, they make around 15000*5 = 75,000. And now when we have home delivery food service companies like Swiggy, Zomato their sales have increased and they make good profits. Now they are planning to start a chain and open a few more stores and increase sales in various areas. The food chain is a good idea for running a business in autopilot mode where we need to put a good setup and keep an employee looking at everything and make some money.

Also,

Housewives earn well by just using their network. Women ask clothing vendors to share their products on their WhatsApp numbers at wholesale prices. And later she just forward the same to her group and network and if anyone is interested to purchase then she just put her margin and gives the order to the clothing vendor and he ships the product. Simple.

Now let's say she gets 150 orders in a month and per order, she earns around 100 Rs profit. Products like Sarees, Kurtis, Hand Bags, etc. So she's making around 150*100 = 15,000Rs monthly profit as a side income.

The journey from earning 50 Paise a day to 2 Lakhs a day: Patricia Narayan - Director, The Sandeepha Chain of Restaurants

From getting rid of a failed marriage, drug addict & abusive husband for taking care of two small kids, Patricia Narayan is the burning example of how to take advantage of hard times instead of being used and controlled by others. She started her business journey by selling samosas, cutlets, and coffee at Marina beach & used to earn 50 Paisa a day & steadily she also started selling hand-made pickles & today due to her decades of hard work she is Director of The Sandeepha chain of Restaurants & earn over 2.5 Lakhs/day.

Her struggles to make the odds meet were difficult, but the courage and determination she showed were extraordinary. In 2010, her struggles and business sense were appreciated and she won the ***FICCI Woman Entrepreneur of the Year*** and soon became an inspiration to all women across the country.

Things are changing and the so-called unstructured or unorganized business in India runs more profitably than most structured organizations. When we talk about Investment and returns than these small unstructured businesses like roadside bookselling, selling samosas, selling chaats like pani puri, selling festivals products like Diwali crackers, Holi Colors, selling vegetables are much more profitable compared to Tier 1 business in which we need a good amount of investments. These small businesses have great Entrepreneurship skills as that single person is the CEO (Chief Executive Officer), CMO (Chief Marketing Officer), and CFO (Chief Financial Officer) of the business. It's a one-man decision. Product or Service discounts or any decision is taken quickly and they don't want to wait for board approvals. One can learn good management lessons from these small businesses. How quickly they adopt the changes, how quickly they make decisions, how quickly they get ideas to grow their business by taking market or area details. The hunger to earn teaches good lessons in small businesses. The new ideas don't take much time. It hardly needs 3-4 weeks to implement those small business ideas and if one of those ideas gets successful then it's a generation business and everyone will get benefitted. Again I am talking about all these because of automation there will be lesser jobs and one needs to prepare for some good alternative source and the young person running for a job could be the next big entrepreneur or even if that person makes a good business than at least his generation would be happy.

"Someone's sitting in the shade today because someone planted a tree a long time ago." — Warren Buffett,

Rightly said, so are we planting a tree for our next generation?

Let's work and bring out good ideas and put your passion as funds and investment and that will surely help enough to start or take the first step towards entrepreneurship. One single idea can make fortunes and miracles. Let's make a choice and become the CEO of a business that is owned by ourselves. Let's work for getting to the next level and work for the next generation. One right choice can make a huge difference for generations and generations.

As Bill Gates put it:

'If you are born poor, it's not your fault. However, if you die poor, that's your fault'.

The reason why I am sharing the Trading and Share Market Mini-Course in the next part of the book is, one can consider trading as a job, as a source of income, as a good opportunity, and if you're having good learning skills then making money from the Share Market doesn't require any rocket science. Consider Trading is like any other Day

Job. We need to work every day, combined with Smart & Hard work, so we get good rewards like Salary & Bonus every year. Some enter the market thinking it's like Speed Money & I can double my Capital every day. This is where disaster strikes. Never get lured into making quick money. Most of the time, you will be out of the Markets pretty soon. Take one day at a time, plan & execute based on Trade setup, never force yourself. Just because another Trader made money... That doesn't mean we can also make it. He got the opportunity & he made use of it. Honestly, he got his Bus, he boarded & he reached his destination. For us, our Bus might come at 10 or 11 or even at 2 PM. Let's wait for our Bus, rather than board a crowded bus which is going to a Different destination.

So I believe that this book is the right bus for you to take you to your destination and help you provide some valuable knowledge.

Let's start…

7. Money Making Opportunities in Trading

Wondering how to become rich from the Share Market? Right?

According to my experience, I can say that we need to improve our skills to grab those money-making opportunities which the Share Market provides us every single day. I firmly believe that when we stay in the Share Market for a long time and do the right things then the Share Market is Supreme and it will surely make justice and provide us unimaginable returns. I have met many silent leaders of the Share Market who are doing wonderful and don't like to be on social media. I got to learn many things from them and sharing my knowledge and experience so others too can learn and take advantage of the opportunity.

Trading and investing in so-called tips or calls or any friend's advice is not the way to stay and make money in the Share Market for a longer time. We need to learn the art of trading to grab those good opportunities. Also, a year or two will get those 2-3 big trades where we will be making a whole year's profit in those 2 trades. That's the opportunities the Share Market provides.

Last year in 2019 when our Finance Minister announced the Corporate Rate Tax cut, that was a huge opportunity when traders made awesome 100-5000% returns trading in options. When we get the opportunity then surely we should hit sixes. But to find those balls to play we need to understand things well and then only we can hit the ball out of the park. We don't need rocket science to find 10-15 good stocks in which we can invest and make good profits. So how to find those stocks and opportunities?

Are you ready? I am happy to see your excitement to learn and get Good Great Knowledge.

So here we go...

8. Trading with Trend line

There are 3 choices to make. And if we can make the right choice then surely will be successful and making huge profits.

When to Buy. When to Sell. When to Seat aside in the Share Market.

To improve our skill of making the right choices we need a good setup and we need to improve our skills to read charts well. I believe that charts speak more than words say. If we are investing in stocks then we need to have knowledge about charts and understand the price actions. As people say **"Price is God"**.

We need to understand the demand and supply areas. Everyone sees the same chart. Everyone sees the same price. Then what's different? Making choice is different.

So how to make the right choices and how to take winning trades?

Well let's see some examples and so we can understand well.

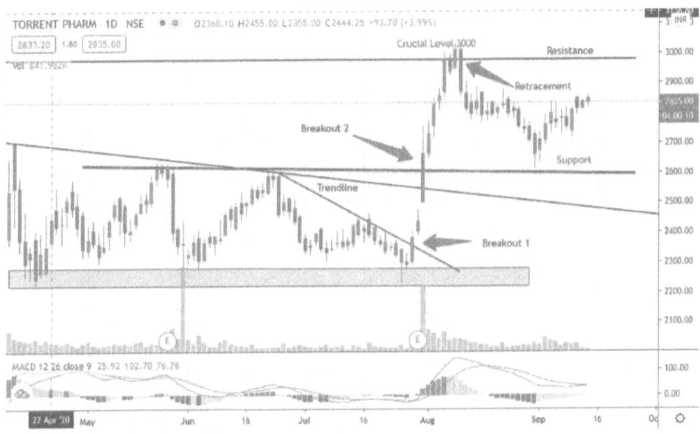

Fig. 5. Torrent Pharma stock chart on a 1-day time frame (*Image Source and Credit: www.tradingview.com*).

As we see in the above fig.5. Torrent Pharma Stock, there are a lot of good money-making opportunities. Now coming to our point of when to buy and when to sell. First will see and try to read the chart. We plotted Horizontal Resistance and Horizontal Support. We plotted trend lines. Now when we saw that our resistance is broken we got an opportunity to enter the trade and bought the shares and sold (we can buy futures and also can trade in options) when we knew that it's respecting the resistance and could retrace back till support.

As we can see at Breakout 1 we had a good opportunity. At breakout 2 we again had a good opportunity. At the resistance level of 3000, we again got a good opportunity to sell the shares. At support levels of 2600, we got a good opportunity to enter again and assumed that the stock will move until our resistance level of 3000. So aren't these opportunities enough?

I will share more examples,

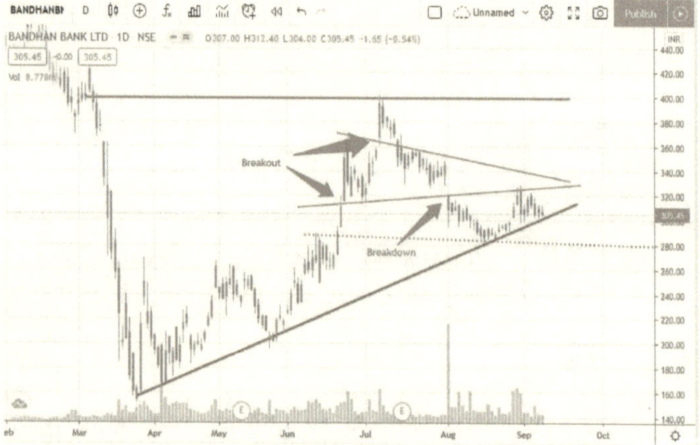

Fig. 6. Bandhan Bank stock chart on a 1-day time frame. (Image Source and Credit: www.tradingview.com).

As we can see in the above fig.6. Bandhan Bank stock, we got a lot of good money-making opportunities. We can see good breakout and breakdown opportunities. Bandhan Bank also respected our resistance levels of 400 and support levels at 320.

Isn't it easy to read the charts and assume the next movement of the stock? Is it that hard?

Hitting a six in cricket is not easy. But good practice and improved skills can make it easy!

Historically, stocks do form the same patterns again and again. Since it works on demand and supply, the resistance and support levels will get respected. Now importantly we need to identify those patterns and be able to identify the right support and resistance areas.

I can say that stocks need some support to bounce back and stocks can take the support of horizontal line supports, trend line supports, moving average supports. We need to identify those areas and with that, we will be able to predict the next moves. Predict means no guarantee but we can assume the future movements of the stock.

Below are some self-explanatory charts and patterns which we need to learn and understand so we can take the trade or make investments accordingly.

Fig. 7. Marico stock chart on a 1-day time frame. (Image Source and Credit: www.tradingview.com).

As we can see in above fig 7. Marico Stock gave a good breakdown at 340 levels, then we got a good head and shoulder pattern, and again upside it made cup & handle pattern. We can also see consolidation areas where a stock makes fewer movements and trades in a range.

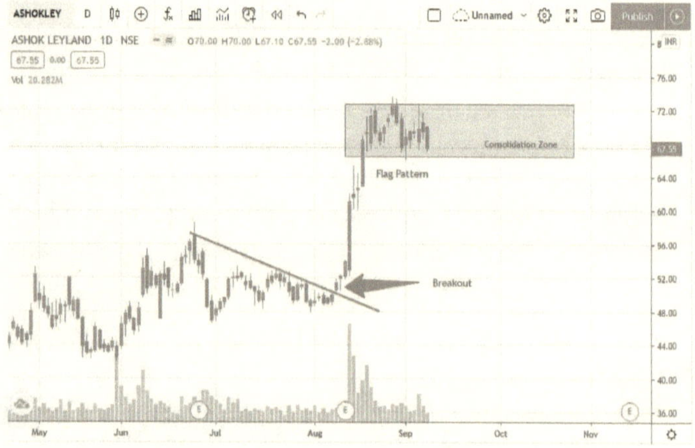

Fig. 8. Ashok Leyland stock chart on a 1-day time frame. (Image Source and Credit: www.tradingview.com).

In the above Fig. 8. Ashok Leyland stock formed a Flag pattern. First, it gave a good breakout of the trend line at 48 and formed a flag pattern. Will wait for our rectangle pattern breakout to take the good money-making opportunity and also we can make a trade and sell Out of the Money Call and Put Options to make money.

Fig. 9. Heromotoco stock chart on a 1-day time frame. (Image Source and Credit: www.tradingview.com).

In above Fig 9. Heromotoco stock trading in Channel pattern. One can take a trade on channel breakout or can invest and hold positions until we see channel breakout. One can use Swing Trading strategies in channel patterns. (For swing trading refer topic)

Fig. 10. Balkrishna Industries stock chart on 15 minutes time frame(Image Source and Credit: www.zerodha.com).

In above fig 10. We can see a sharp 50 points fall in Balkrishna Industries in Intraday and it was a good money-making opportunity. It was a good Symmetrical triangle pattern breakout trade. The market lot size of Balkrishna Industries in Futures is 800 and so with single lot trade, we would have a made 800*50 = 40,000 profit. (Futures trading refer topic)

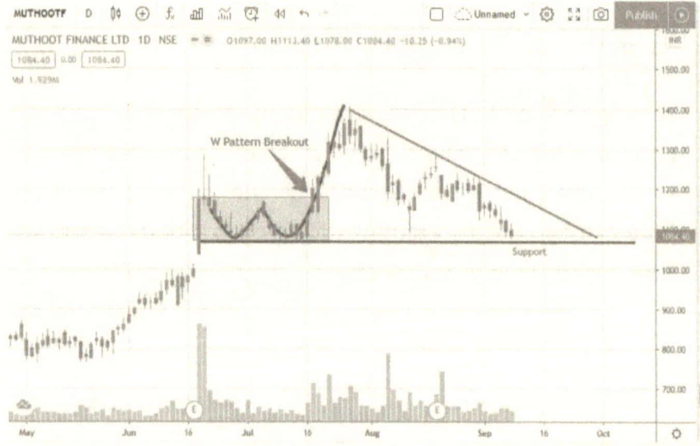

Fig. 11. Muthoot Finance stock chart on a 1-day time frame. (Image Source and Credit: www.tradingview.com).

In Fig. 11 Muthoot Finance gave a good breakout in the Rectangle W pattern and formed a descending triangle pattern. Now one can get another opportunity when it breaks the support on the downside or when it breaks the trend line resistance on the upside.

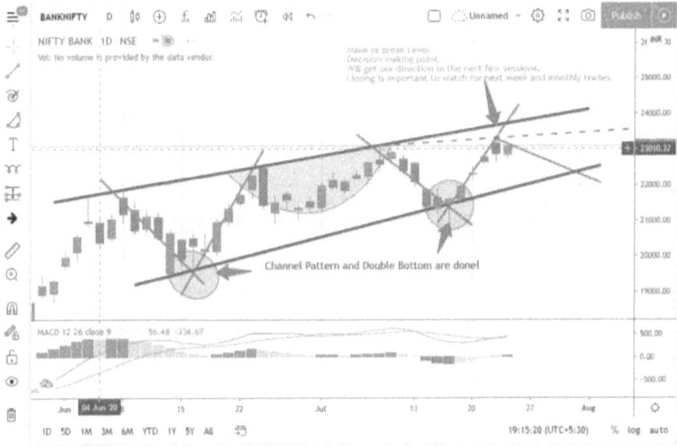

Fig. 12. Bank Nifty stock chart on a 1-day time frame. (Image Source and Credit: www.tradingview.com).

In above Fig. 12 Bank Nifty made a Double bottom pattern and we plotted trend lines to get Bank Nifty further movement and were expecting it to respect our Trend lines and fall till support levels or if it falls with volumes then can expect to break support levels and fall more giving good money-making opportunity.

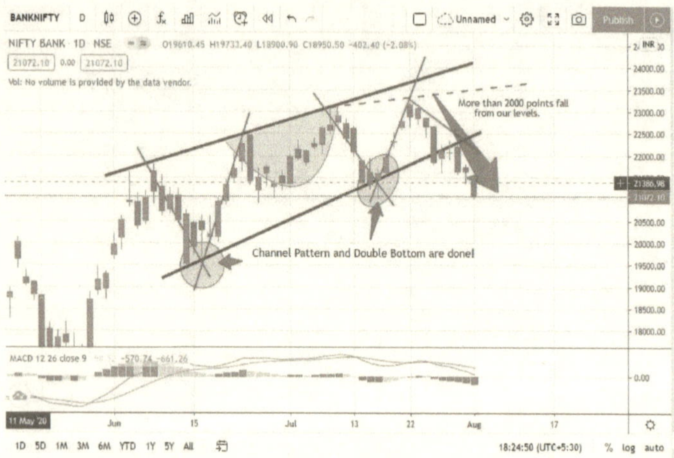

Fig. 13. Bank Nifty stock chart on a 1-day time frame.(Image Source and Credit: www.tradingview.com).

As we can see above Fig. 13 Bank Nifty respected our levels and pattern and gave us good 2000 points from 23000 to 21000 within 7-8 trading sessions. It was a good Double bottom pattern breakout in Bank Nifty.

Fig. 14. Bank Nifty stock chart on 3 minutes time frame (Image Source and Credit: www.tradingview.com).

In the above Fig. 14 on Intraday Bank Nifty gave good Trend line breakout. Horizontal Support and Trend line resistance were well respected and later it gave good big trade when we saw a breakout on the upside.

Fig. 15. Reliance stock chart on 5 minutes time frame (Image Source and Credit: www.zerodha.com).

As seen in the above Fig. 15 Reliance stock formed a good W pattern and gave a beautiful breakout on the Horizontal resistance line and we got another good trade at trend line breakout.

Now we got the chart patterns and understood how patterns work and what are trading opportunities at the breakouts and with this chart analysis, we can make future predictions (predictions mean not a guarantee but assumptions) of any stock. But what are entry and exit points? When to buy and when to sell?

Let's see that,

9. Trading Style and Methods

Every person has his trading style and methods. One can't copy another's exact method or style. So what I will advise is to take examples and create and improve your own trading styles.

Just like in Cricket, every player is a master of his skills. Some are aggressive cricketers or good in 2020 formats, some are defensive or good test players. Similarly, we need to apply that in Trading in the Share Market.

Let's take an example of 3 traders and their trading styles.

Trader 1: Aggressive Trader

The aggressive trader enters the trade as soon as stocks make a breakout on the same candle. The advantage of this method is he gets all profit from breakout to next moves. And the disadvantage of this method is he doesn't get any breakout confirmation.

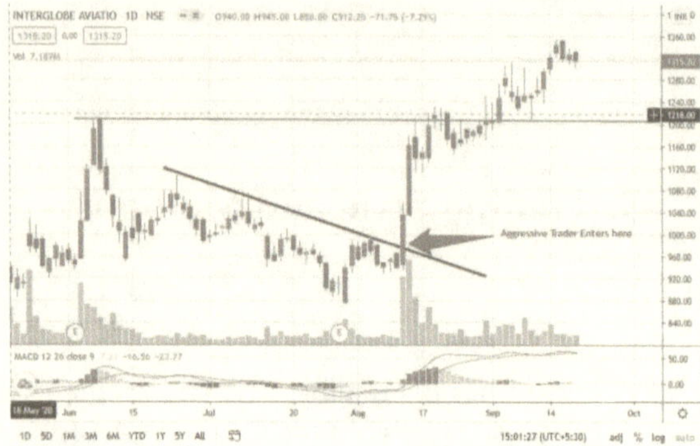

Fig. 16. Indigo stock chart on a 1-day time frame. (Image Source and Credit: www.tradingview.com).

Trader 2: Confirmative Trader

The confirmative trader trades only when he gets trade confirmation. In breakout when the first candle high is broken then he will take the trade. The advantage of this method is he gets trade confirmation. And the disadvantage of this method is that the first candle can be big and he will miss that profit.

Fig. 17. Indigo stock chart on a 1-day time frame.(Image Source and Credit: www.tradingview.com).

Trader 3: Patience Trader

Patience trader trades on a pullback of stock to the breakout line. When the stock makes a breakout and gets back to the breakout line and then he takes the trade. The disadvantage of this method is that if the stock doesn't get back to the breakout line then he won't be able to take the trade.

Fig. 18. Pidilite Industries stock chart on a 1-day time frame. (Image Source and Credit: www.tradingview.com).

So which method is better? You can choose the best which suits you. I prefer the second method of Confirmative Trader.

Time Frame:

According to my experience, I can say that higher time frames are more reliable and good for patterns. Long-term time frames provide us future targets and the direction of the stock. Short-term time frames provide us entry and exit points. Long term time frame means monthly, weekly, or daily time frames. Short-term time frame means 15mins or 5mins time frames for our setup.

One should avoid trading on a 1min time frame unless one has good experience of trading. A short-term time frame like 1min or 3min can form false signals.

So now when we can read and understand (analyze) charts we can take winning trades. But in which segment? Equity, Futures, or Options? Which is safer? Which segment needs less investment? Which segment will give huge returns? So many questions right? So here we got with basic difference in all three segments,

Let's take an example,

In the Equity Cash segment, to buy Reliance 1010 shares at share price 2200 will need a capital of 22,22,000 Rs.

In Futures Segment, to buy Reliance Futures with 1010 shares will need a capital of around 6 lakhs.

In the Options Segment, will need a capital of 50,000 to 75,000 depending on options strike price and premium. (Strike price and the premium will discuss further in options, don't get confused).

So from an investment perspective Futures and Options looks good. Right? So are you ready to learn more about Futures and Options?

Let's divine to learn about Futures and Options.

10. Derivatives Trading

Futures and Options are called Derivatives in the Share Market.

Since Futures & Options are derived from the underlying assets like Stocks, Index, and Commodities. For example, Mango juice is derived from Mango only and Apple juice is derived from Apple only. Similarly from a particular stock, we derive Futures and Options from that stock only. From Reliance we can take Reliance Futures and Reliance Options trades.

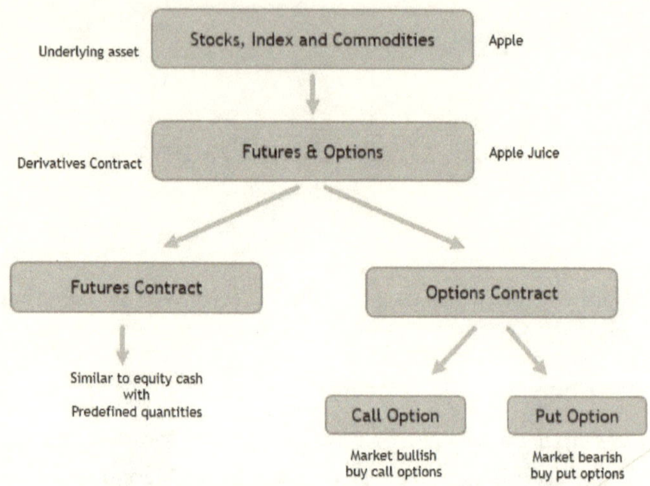

Fig. 20. Derivatives Trading.

In the derivatives market there are two types of contracts:

1. **Futures Contract**

2. **Options Contract**

Futures contracts are similar to Equity cash. There is only two difference in the Futures contract and Equity cash.

- Futures contracts have an expiry.

- Futures contracts have fixed predefined quantities.

In the Equity cash market, in Reliance stock we can buy or sell 1, 2, 3 N number of shares. But if we are buying Reliance Futures then we can buy only in predefined quantities. Reliance predefined quantity is 505, Nifty Index predefined quantity is 75 and Bank Nifty Index predefined quantity is 25. And we cannot customize that, instead, we need to buy in multiples of those quantities.

Similarly, in Options Contract we can buy or sell predefined quantities. But if the same number of shares we can buy in the equity cash market then why do we need Futures and Options. Right?

I will tell you why.

Why Futures and Options are introduced?

Futures and Options are used for hedging purposes and they are predominantly used by FII's and DII's. Now, what is hedging?

I will share an example of hedging so you can understand it well. Suppose if we buy a house of 50 lakhs with an EMI option. Now we are paying a monthly EMI of 25,000 Rs. To minimize that EMI expense we can rent our ground or first floor at 15,000Rs so that will reduce our total EMI cost (25,000 – 15,000 = 10,000).

So now the total amount we spend is only 10,000Rs. This management is called hedging.

Will take an example of Reliance stock. Suppose we have bought 1000 shares of Reliance at 2000Rs each. Now our investment is 1000*2000 = 20,00,000 Rs. Now if there is a temporary loss in share price then will make a big loss. If there are some legal issues with Reliance Company or any bad news or MD getting resign or bad quarterly results then the share price might go down and will make a loss.

In this case, now Reliance share price gets to 1500, and with 1500 share price will make a loss of 500*1000 = 5,00,000RS. Our portfolio will now show us a loss of 5 lakh and so to minimize this loss we can take a counter position in Futures and Options. That means, we can sell Reliance Futures or Buy Put Option or Sell Call Option. So that we can make a profit of 4-5 lakhs from Futures and Options in counter positions and our portfolio will have less loss or no loss. This is called hedging.

It is used by Mutual Funds who are having huge investments in Equity cash markets and they hedge their positions with Futures and Options.

Futures Trading

Futures contracts are organized and made by the exchange. It's safe because it's regulated by the exchange. Now talking about futures contracts then we need to understand some technical words and things.

If futures contracts are trading lesser price than the spot price then we call it Discount.

For example, the Reliance share price is trading at 2200 and the Reliance Future price is trading at 2150. Here the reliance future price is trading at 50 points less and it's called a discount.

If futures contracts are trading higher prices than the spot price then we call it Premium.

For example, the Reliance share price is trading at 2200 and the Reliance Future price is trading at 2250. Here the reliance future price is trading at 50 points more and it's called the premium.

On expiry, we can see futures price and spot price to be equal.

Options Trading

Options trading is a high-risk high-return business.

Let's take an example to understand in a better way. In this Covid-19 pandemic, many people are afraid and think that they might need Health Insurance. So for an emergency, they will take a Health Insurance of let's say for example 1 Crore Rupees Health Insurance. Now to get that Health Insurance they will visit an Insurance company.

Now the Insurance Company will ask customers to pay some monthly or quarterly premiums to get that insurance based on their period and probability ratio of getting an emergency. So, to get 1 Crore Rupees Health Insurance customers will need to pay 1000 Rupees monthly premium for the next 5 years. Now here, the Insurance Company is the Options Seller and the Customer is the Option Buyer. Now we need to understand what risk-reward is for both of them and what the mindset is.

The customer thinks for 1 Crore he needs to pay a small premium and so it's no big risk and requires less investment for a big reward. And the Insurance Company thinks that all customers won't need Insurance in that period so they will be in profits if the number of people getting an emergency is less.

But, when all customers would require an emergency then the Insurance Company will be in huge loss and the Customer will be in big profit. Right? But, according to my experience, I can say that Option Seller makes more times profit than Option Buyer. Out of 10 times, 8 times Options Seller makes money. Why? Let me finish the options part for that :)

In options trading, we need to trade in Call and Put Options. We buy a call option when the market or stock is bullish and we buy a put option when the market or stock is bearish.

Let's take an example,

Suppose Reliance is trading at 2000 price and we are expecting Reliance to go up till 2200 price. In this case, we will buy the 2000 or 2100 or 2200 strike price Call option.

i.e. Reliance Sept 2200 CE

So in the above example, we have taken the Reliance stock Call option of September month expiry with a strike price of 2200.

And if we are expecting Reliance to go down below 2000 then we will buy 2000 or 1900 or 1800 strike price Put option.

i.e. Reliance Sept 1800 PE

When the Reliance price will increase at that time Reliance call option price will also increase and the option buyer will make a profit. And when the Reliance price will decrease at that time Reliance put option price will increase and the option buyer will make a profit.

Basic terminologies used in Options:

- **Strike price -**Strike price is the price per share for which the underlying security may be purchased or sold by the option holder. (Will cover this in-depth in Option Chain in the next chapter)

- **Option price/premium -**It is the price for which the option buyer pays to the seller.

- **Expiration Day -**The day on which a derivatives contract ceases to exist. For Index Options, Options expire every Thursday in weekly options. For Monthly Options, Options expire on the last Thursday of the month.

- **Spot Price -**It is the price at which the underlying asset trades in the spot market.

- **Open Interest -**Open Interest is the total number of option contracts outstanding for any underlying asset.

Best Setup: Strong Technical and Strong Fundamentals

On 22nd June 2020, Glenmark Pharma gave huge returns Intraday. 15mins time frame chart gave a good ascending triangle breakout. And options Glenmark Pharma jumped to give 5000+% returns with strong fundamental news of Covid-19 vaccine from Glenmark company.

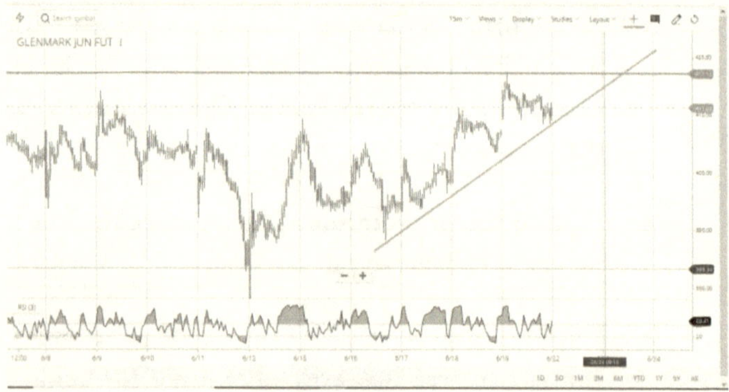

Fig. 21. Glenmark Pharma stock chart on 15 minutes time frame.(Image Source and Credit: www.zerodha.com).

Big trade opportunities when we see good technical and fundamental work at a time. Glenmark in options trading gave good returns of more than 5000%.

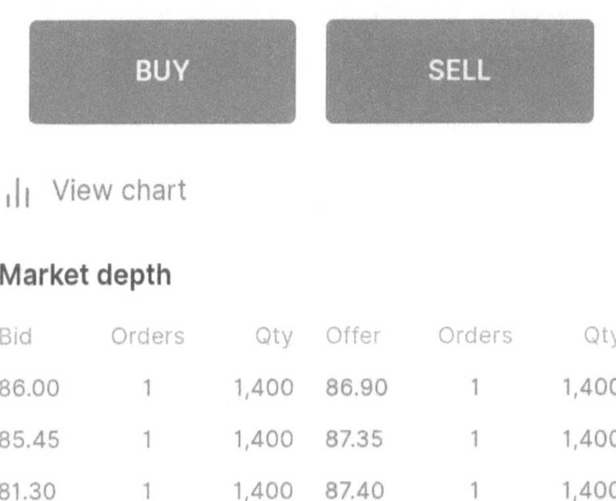

Fig. 22. Glenmark Pharma Call Option Chart. (Image Source and Credit: www.zerodha.com).

Now to buy a Glenmark Call option of 460 strike price at a premium of 8 Rs we need an investment of 1400*8 = 11200 Rs (Lot size for Glenmark is 1400 shares). And when we sell at 80 Rs we earn around 100800Rs profit. That is a 1000% return. The call option the previous day's close was 1.60 Rs and made a high of 86 Rs.

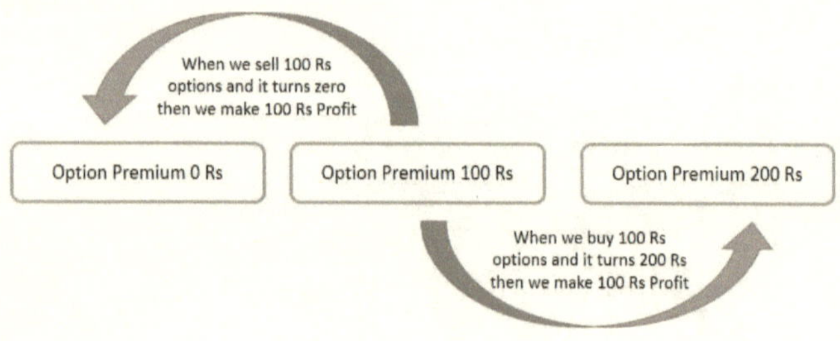

Fig. 23. Options Trading.

How to select a strike price? How to see what is the premium?

Let's learn the option chain for that…

11. Option Chain and Data Analysis

Option Chain is the most useful tool for any Futures and Options trader. Option Chain is a table that contains all the options data in a specific format as follows:

- It consists of all the Call Options and Put Options (Strikes) available for trading.

- Total Open Interest (Outstanding Open Positions) for every Option contract.

- Intrinsic Volatility (Change in Option's price with a change in underlying security) for every Option Contract.

- Change in Open Interest on a particular day.

- Trading Volume of each Option Contact on a particular day.

As I've said earlier Option Chain is the most useful tool for Futures & Options traders now I'll explain how to use it. Now as we know that Open Interest is the total number of Open/Outstanding positions in an option contract we can predict support and resistance levels for any security (Index or Stock). You will understand how we can predict exact support and resistance levels using the Option Chain below.

- The put options are sold by people who are bullish on the Index or Stock. As the Index or Stock goes up Put Options lose their value and put option sellers (writers) make money.

- So the Put Option has the highest Open Interest is expected to be the best Support level for the Index or Stock.

- Similarly, the Call Option is sold by people who are bearish about the Index or Stock. As the Index or Stock goes down the Call Options lose their value and sellers (writers) make money.

- So the Call Option having the highest Open Interest is expected to be the strongest Resistance level for the Index or Stock.

Now the question is, how you can earn a profit from this information?

Whenever we see the Index or Stock is trading substantially higher than the Strike Price of the Call Option having the highest OI then you go short on the Index or Stock.

Similarly, if you see the Index or Stock is trading substantially lower than the Strike Price of the Put Option having the highest OI then you go long on the Stock or Index.

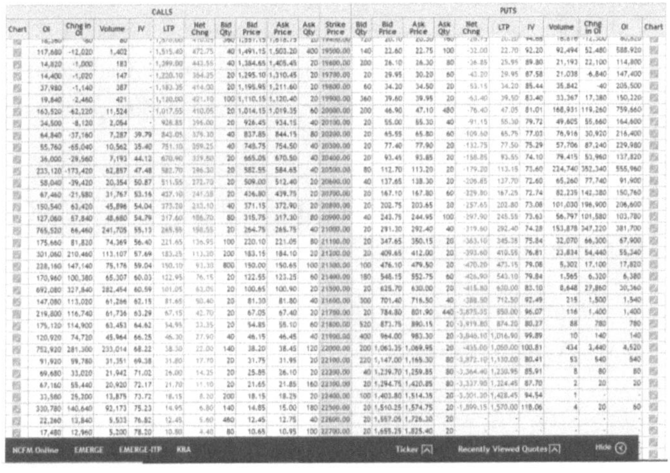

CALLS

OI	Chng in OI	Volume	IV	LTP	Net Chng	Bid Qty	Bid Price	Ask Price	Ask Qty	Strike Price
[illegible]	[illegible]	80	-	1,570.00	410.[illegible]	360	1,551.15	1,618.75	20	19400.00
117,680	-12,020	1,402	-	1,515.40	472.75	40	1,491.15	1,503.20	400	19500.00
14,820	-1,000	183	-	1,399.00	443.55	40	1,384.65	1,405.45	20	19600.00
14,400	-1,020	147	-	1,220.10	364.25	20	1,295.10	1,310.45	20	19700.00
37,980	-1,140	387	-	1,183.35	414.00	20	1,195.95	1,211.60	20	19800.00
19,840	-2,460	421	-	1,120.00	421.10	100	1,110.15	1,120.40	20	19900.00
163,520	-62,220	11,524	-	1,017.55	410.05	20	1,014.15	1,019.35	60	20000.00
34,500	-8,120	2,064	-	926.85	396.00	20	926.45	934.15	40	20100.00
64,840	-37,160	7,287	39.79	843.05	379.10	40	837.85	844.15	80	20200.00
55,760	-65,040	10,562	35.40	751.10	359.25	40	748.75	754.50	40	20300.00
36,000	-29,560	7,193	44.12	670.90	339.50	20	665.05	670.50	40	20400.00
233,120	-173,420	62,857	47.48	582.70	296.30	20	582.55	584.65	40	20500.00
58,040	-39,420	20,354	50.87	511.55	272.70	20	509.00	512.40	20	20600.00
67,460	-21,580	31,767	53.16	437.10	241.58	20	436.80	439.75	20	20700.00
150,540	63,420	45,896	54.04	373.20	213.10	40	371.15	372.90	20	20800.00
127,060	57,840	48,680	54.79	317.60	186.70	80	315.75	317.30	80	20900.00
765,520	66,460	241,705	55.13	265.55	198.55	20	264.75	265.75	40	21000.00
175,660	81,820	74,369	56.40	221.65	136.95	100	220.10	221.05	80	21100.00
301,060	210,460	113,107	57.69	183.45	113.30	200	183.15	184.10	20	21200.00
228,160	147,140	75,176	59.04	150.10	91.30	800	150.00	150.65	100	21300.00
170,960	100,380	65,307	60.03	122.95	76.15	20	122.55	123.25	60	21400.00
692,080	327,840	282,454	60.59	101.05	63.05	20	100.65	100.90	20	21500.00
147,080	113,020	61,286	62.15	81.65	50.40	20	81.30	81.80	40	21600.00
219,800	116,740	61,736	63.29	67.15	42.70	20	67.05	67.40	20	21700.00
175,120	114,900	63,453	64.62	54.95	33.35	20	54.85	55.10	60	21800.00
120,920	74,720	45,964	66.25	46.30	27.90	40	46.15	46.45	40	21900.00
752,920	281,300	233,014	68.22	38.30	22.00	140	38.20	38.45	120	22000.00
91,920	99,780	31,351	69.38	31.80	17.70	20	31.75	31.95	20	22100.00
69,680	33,020	21,942	71.02	26.00	14.35	20	25.85	26.10	20	22200.00
67,160	55,440	20,920	72.17	21.70	11.10	20	21.65	21.85	160	22300.00
33,580	25,200	13,875	73.72	18.15	8.20	200	18.15	18.25	20	22400.00
330,780	140,640	92,173	75.23	14.95	6.80	140	14.85	15.00	180	22500.00
22,260	13,840	5,533	76.82	12.45	5.60	460	12.45	12.75	40	22600.00
17,480	12,960	5,200	78.20	10.80	4.40	80	10.65	10.95	100	22700.00

PUTS

Strike Price	Bid Qty	Bid Price	Ask Price	Ask Qty	Net Chng	LTP	IV	Volume	Chng in OI	OI
19400.00	720	40.10	20.30	160	-20.73	20.30	94.66	16,816	-12,300	80,520
19500.00	140	22.60	22.75	100	-32.00	22.70	92.20	92,494	52,480	588,920
19600.00	200	26.10	26.30	80	-26.85	25.95	89.80	21,193	22,100	114,800
19700.00	20	29.95	30.20	60	-43.20	29.95	87.58	21,038	-6,840	147,400
19800.00	60	34.20	34.50	20	53.15	34.20	85.44	35,842	-40	205,500
19900.00	360	39.60	39.95	20	-63.40	39.50	83.40	33,367	17,380	150,220
20000.00	200	46.90	47.10	480	-76.40	47.05	81.01	168,931	119,260	759,660
20100.00	20	55.00	55.30	40	-91.15	55.30	79.72	49,605	55,660	164,600
20200.00	20	45.55	65.80	60	-109.60	65.75	77.03	76,916	30,920	216,400
20300.00	20	77.40	77.90	20	-132.75	77.50	75.29	57,706	87,240	229,980
20400.00	20	93.45	93.85	20	-158.85	93.55	74.10	79,415	53,960	137,820
20500.00	80	112.70	113.20	20	-179.20	113.15	73.60	224,740	352,340	555,960
20600.00	40	137.65	138.30	20	-206.65	137.70	72.60	65,260	77,740	91,900
20700.00	20	167.10	167.80	60	-229.80	167.25	72.74	82,235	142,380	150,760
20800.00	20	202.75	203.65	20	-257.65	202.80	73.08	101,030	196,900	206,600
20900.00	40	243.75	244.95	100	-297.90	245.55	73.63	56,797	101,580	103,780
21000.00	20	291.30	292.40	40	-319.60	292.40	74.28	153,878	347,220	381,700
21100.00	20	347.65	350.15	20	-363.10	345.35	75.84	32,070	66,300	67,900
21200.00	20	409.65	412.00	20	-393.60	410.55	76.81	23,834	54,440	55,340
21300.00	100	476.10	479.50	20	-470.20	473.15	79.08	5,302	17,100	17,820
21400.00	180	548.15	552.75	60	-426.90	543.10	79.84	1,565	6,320	6,380
21500.00	20	625.70	630.00	20	-415.80	630.00	83.10	8,648	27,860	30,360
21600.00	300	701.40	716.50	40	-388.50	712.50	92.49	215	1,500	1,540
21700.00	20	784.80	801.90	440	-3,875.35	850.00	96.07	116	1,400	1,400
21800.00	520	871.75	890.15	20	-3,919.80	874.20	80.27	88	780	780
21900.00	400	964.00	983.30	20	-3,846.10	1,016.90	99.89	10	140	140
22000.00	200	1,061.35	1,069.95	20	-435.00	1,050.00	100.81	434	3,440	4,520
22100.00	220	1,147.00	1,165.30	80	-3,972.10	1,130.00	80.41	53	540	540
22200.00	40	1,239.70	1,259.85	80	-3,364.40	1,230.95	85.91	8	80	80
22300.00	20	1,294.75	1,420.85	80	-3,337.95	1,324.45	87.70	2	20	20
22400.00	100	1,403.80	1,514.35	20	-3,301.30	1,428.45	94.54	1	-	-
22500.00	20	1,510.25	1,574.75	20	-1,899.15	1,570.00	118.06	4	20	60
22600.00	20	1,557.05	1,726.30	20	-	-	-	-	-	-
22700.00	20	1,695.25	1,825.40	20	-	-	-	-	-	-

Fig. 24. Options Chain. (Image Source: www.nseindia.com)

In the NSEIndia website option chain table, all the strike prices in the yellow color background in Call and Put side are In the Money (ITM) strike prices, and all the strike prices with a white color background in call and put side are Out of the Money (OTM) strike prices.

As a simple example, suppose I am traveling from Delhi to Bangalore by train and right now I am standing at the station Mumbai. The stations which I have already crossed are known as In the Money stations and the stations which are yet to cross are known as Out of the Money. And the station at which I am standing right now is called At the Money (ATM).

Let's say for example Bank Nifty is trading at a price of 20000 and so below 20000 prices, all strike prices in the Call side are In the Money strike prices as 19900, 19800, and above 20000 prices all strike prices in the Call side are Out of the Money strike prices. And the 20000 prices are called as At the Money.

At expiry, all Out of the Money strike prices premium turns zero.

Options Prices depend on Option Greeks (Delta, Theta, Vega, Gamma).

Now the important and watchful point is Premium Decay. What's premium decay and how it helps us to make a profit?

We need to understand the effect of premium decay on various strike prices like In the Money, At the Money, and Out of the Money. As we know all Out of the Money premium turns zero on expiry and so the effect of premium decay on Out of the Money strike prices is more compared to In the Money and At the Money. Option Seller takes the advantage of premium decay and makes a profit when the premium of the option gets decreased.

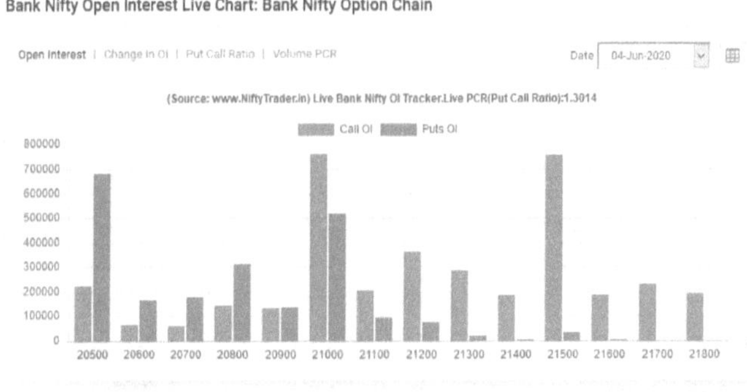

Fig. 25. Open Interest Chart of Bank Nifty. (Image Source and Credit: www.niftytrader.in.com).

Being able to analyze the data allows traders to make better-informed trading decisions. In data analysis, we need to understand long buildup, short buildup, short-covering, and long unwinding.

Long Buildup:

People create long positions when they are expecting the price of the stock to go up. An increase in Open Interest and Price will give us an idea of Long Buildup and traders are expecting the price to go up in the near term.

Short Buildup:

People create short positions when they are expecting the price of the stock to go down. An increase in Open Interest and a decrease in Price will give us an idea of Short Buildup and traders are expecting the price to go down in the near term.

Short Covering:

It's interesting and very useful and we have seen professional traders taking good advantage of Short Covering rallies. People who have short positions will buy the position and shorts will get covered. The Price will increase and Open Interest will decrease indicating short covering. Will take an example here of Bank Nifty.

Suppose Bank Nifty is trading at 21300 and people have sold 21500 Call Option at a price of 100 Rs and when Bank Nifty starts trading at 21800 then that trader will have a loss in position and he will square off the position and will buy the position and when so many positions will get covered at a time then we can expect a good short-covering rally on upside.

Long Unwinding: People who have long positions will sell the position. Open Interest and Price will decrease indicating long unwinding. Long unwinding causes the stock to go down.

Stock or Market moves up either by long buildup or short coverings and stock or Market moves down either by short buildup or long unwinding's. We need to analyze those data to understand if the market or stock is having good strong buying or selling pressures.

We often see good short-covering rallies in Index like Nifty and Bank Nifty and we can get good trading opportunities on those good short-covering rallies to make money!

12. Options Buying Vs Options Selling

There is always a debate about whether to be an option buyer or option seller and which is better. I would say that rather than becoming just an option buyer or option seller, we need to be an option play to make good money from options trading.

The below table shows us the difference between options buying and options selling.

Options Buying	Options Selling
Less Capital Required	More Capital Required
Loss limited to premium	Loss is unlimited
Profit Unlimited	Profit limited
Needs market to be trendy	Needs range-bound market
Time is enemy	Time is friend
Needs chart	Needs option data
The preferred trading method is Scalping	The preferred trading method is Positional

Benefits of Options Buying

1. Options give you the power of Leveraging, as with limited capital one can ride the bigger move.

2. The Risk involved here is to the tune of Premium paid. Say, if someone is buying a Nifty call option by paying a premium of 40. And a Nifty lot consists of 75 units. Therefore, the total premium paid will be equal to 40*75 = Rs. 3,000. So, by paying a premium of Rs. 3000 one can ride the full move.

3. The option buyer has the opportunity of earning unlimited profit by just paying a premium and the loss is limited to the premium invested.

Benefits of Options Selling

To understand this, let us understand the scenarios option contracts move to at expiry:

1. When the Spot price moves above the strike price at expiry, the option expires In The Money. Options buyer's gains and makes money.

2. When the Spot price is at or near the strike price at expiry, the option expires At The Money. The Option seller earns the premium received as his income as the contract expires worthless for the buyer.

3. When the Spot price is below the strike at expiry, the option expires Out Of Money. The Options

sellers earn the premium received as income as the contract expires worthless for the buyer.

So, from the three scenarios mentioned above, the Option Buyer makes money in one of the scenarios and the option seller stands to make money in two scenarios.

Option buying is safer than option selling but if the market or stock is consolidating then option buying will lead to frustration and losses.

When underlying moves in a violent way option buying are the best.

Option buying returns are unmatchable to option selling when there is high volatility in the market or stock.

In options, buying returns are so high sometimes more than 5000 % also. (Refer Topic)

Suppose if we sell an option for 100 Rs premium then our maximum profit is 100rs premium but the risk is unlimited theoretically whereas if we buy the option of 100 Rs then the loss is limited to 100 Rs and profit can be unlimited as it can turn to 200, 500 or 1000 also.

In option buying margin requirements is low.

- Risk is low but the probability of profit is also low.

- In option buying we want the move to be fast and large.

- Whereas option selling with strategies can give high probability profit and stable income. With good options strategies, we can make money even if the market is trading against us by using spreads and counter positions.

- Risk-defined option strategies are the best if you have high capital.

- I know traders who make money daily by option buying and also by options selling.

- Both option buying and option selling can mint money but we will have to be more disciplined and follow our strategies and setup well.

- Both option buying and option selling have their advantages and disadvantages to choose the side of your personality suits.

We need to be options players rather than just being an option buyer or option seller!

So what are those good options and futures strategies?

Let's learn...

13. Three Market Trends

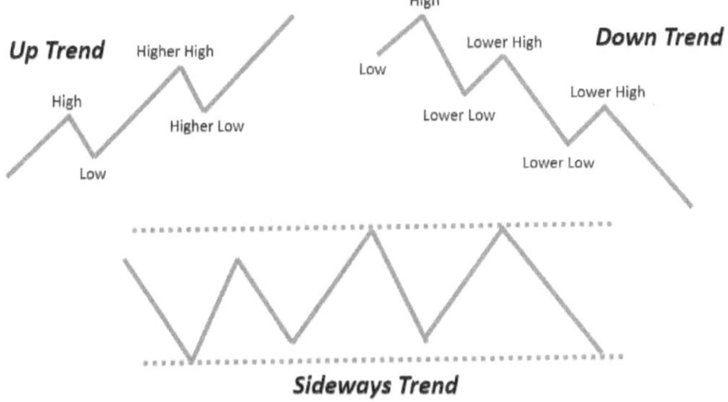

Fig. 26. Market Trends.

Trading along with the Trend is the simple and the best method!

"The trend is your friend until the end when it bends."

There are three trends in the market as we can see in above fig 26. Up Trend, Down Trend, and Sideways Trend.

It's been highlighted and said by many successful traders to trade with the trend because it's a good opportunity and core of successful trading.

Still, traders do take trades against the trend. Why?

It's highly dependent on individual analysis and trading style and everyone differs from one another. Traders do make some money by going against the trend and try to be different from the crowd.

Now does that mean that you will never lose money by trading with the trend? Of course not! Every trend ends and reverses eventually which will stop you out. Furthermore, markets make regular pullbacks as a part of an ongoing trend that could stop you from prematurely.

We should always trade with the trend until it hurts. One must Paper trade it. I think you'll be pleased with the results by trading with and against the trend. One of the things that the majority of folk's find most challenging about trading is determining which is more important: a good entry or a good exit?

According to my, the three components of good trading are market analysis, money management, and mental attitude.

There is a world of difference between paper trading and real trading. And the difference is the emotional impact trading has on us when we trade with real money.

Emotions make a trader hang on to a losing trade because he has the hope that the market will turn around and get him back to break even, causing him to ride a bad trade into oblivion.

Emotions will keep a trader out of entering a perfectly good trade because he is afraid of this being a losing trade.

Emotions make a trader exit a good trade, right after he entered because the normal jiggles in price make him doubtful of his analysis and afraid of losing on this trade, thus making him miss out on what could be a long ride. Trades are rarely entered at the low point of a V-shaped bottom. This applies to both position trades and day trades. The time frames may be different (days, in case of a position trade, and minutes, in case of a day-trade), but the principle is the same: What looked like a perfectly well-thought-out trade before the order was placed can turn into a struggle with fear and doubt. Once these emotions surface, it becomes difficult to stick with the original plan. A carelessly placed entry almost always results in a bad trade.

On the other hand, take those incidences when a buy was made right at the low. What a nice and relaxed feeling, when the market goes in the right direction immediately after entry! So what, if there are some wiggles! There is a profit, even if it's only a small profit. Now it is so much easier to keep a cool head and make the right decision. Therefore, I believe that a trader should strive to perfect his entry techniques first, and worry about the exit later on.

Here are some tips for the newcomer, aimed at relieving trading stress:

- Use stop-loss! Many traders trade without stop-loss. They argue that they don't need to place stop-loss orders because they are closely monitoring the market. This may be so, but the intense monitoring required, and the ever-present possibility of a quick adverse price move, create unnecessary additional stress. A well-placed stop-loss can do a lot to relieve the tension associated with a new position.

- Keep your positions small! Many newcomers try to make a quick killing by using positions that are too large for their account or trading a stock that's too volatile for them. A sure way to increase the stress level!

- Accept yourself for what you are! There are many ways to trade the markets. But we all have different personalities, and many trading styles simply don't fit our personality and emotional set-up.

- Some people are natural long-term investors; some people are natural day-traders. Find out what suits you best. And then jump to practice those and hit sixes once you master those great skills!

14. Trading Strategies

I believe that people make their own luck with great preparation and good strategy.

-Jack Canfield

I completely agree with this quote by Jack Canfield. We need great preparation and good strategies in trading to make professional things work well and we get good returns consistently. As trading is not gambling and we are not in a casino.

Till now we understood the basics and chart reading and once we can assume the stock or market directions, it's time to work on strategies that will give us good trade and right risk management.

Let's start with some good and amazing strategies,

A) Neutral Market Strategies

We use neutral market strategies when we are expecting a good move in stock or market in either direction or no movement at all i.e. flat market.

Big movement | Options Buying:

Strategies called Long Straddle or Long Strangle can be used when we are expecting a big move in the market or stock in either direction (either up or down) because of any event like the budget announcement, policy announcements from RBI, company quarterly results, or elections results or any news by which stock or market can make a good move and we are not sure of the direction.

To set up these strategies we need to buy both Call and Put options.

When we buy Call and Put options of the same strike price of At the Money strike price then it's called Long Straddle Strategies.

Buy ATM CE and Buy ATM PE

And, when we buy Call and Put options of the same price with different strike prices like Out of the Money strike price options then it's called Long Strangle Strategies.

Buy OTM CE and Buy OTM PE

Flat or Sideways Movement | Options Selling:

Strategies called Short Straddle or Short Strangle can be used when we are expecting a flat or sideways movement in the market or stock.

To set up these strategies we need to sell both Call and Put options.

When we sell Call and Put options of the same strike price of At the Money strike price then it's called Short Straddle Strategies.

Sell ATM CE and Sell ATM PE

And, when we sell Call and Put options of the same price with different strike prices like Out of the Money strike price options then it's called Short Strangle Strategies.

Sell OTM CE and Sell OTM PE

B) Bull Market Strategies

We use bull market strategies when we are expecting a stock or market to move in an upside direction i.e. bullish trend.

There are good four strategies when we are expecting stock or market to move in the upside direction.

Bull Call Spread

The bull call spread strategy is employed when you think that the price of the stock will go up moderately in the near term.

Bull call spread can be implemented by buying an in-the-money call option also by writing a higher striking OTM call option of the same stock.

Buy 1 ITM Call and Sell 1 OTM Call

Bull Put Spread

The bull put spread option strategy is entered when the options trader thinks that the price of the stock will go up moderately in the near term.

Bull call spreads can be implemented by selling an in-the-money put option also by writing a lower striking OTM put option of the same stock.

Sell 1 ITM Put and Buy 1 OTM Put

Long Call Option

The long call option strategy is the most basic options trading strategy where we buy a call option.

These are very easy to set up since it's just a single option order.

BUY 1 ATM Call

Short Put Option

A trader is expecting a steady or rising stock price during the life of the option. The only real goal for writing an uncovered Put is to earn the premium as income.

These are very easy to set up since it's just a single option order.

Sell 1 OTM Put

C) Bear Market Strategies

We use bear market strategies when we are expecting stock or market to move in the downside direction i.e. bearish trend.

There are good four strategies when we are expecting stock or market to move in the upside direction.

Bear Call Spread

The bear call spread option trading strategy is employed when the options trader thinks that the price of the stock will go down in the near term.

Bear call spreads can be implemented by buying call options of a certain strike price and selling the same number of call options of the lower strike price.

Buy 1 OTM Call and Sell 1 ITM Call

Bear Put Spread

The bear put spread option trading strategy is employed when the options trader thinks that the price of the asset will go down moderately.

Bear put spreads can be implemented by buying a higher striking in the money put option and selling a lower striking out of the money put option of the stock.

Buy 1 ITM Put and Sell 1 OTM Put

Long Put Option

The long put option strategy is the second most basic options trading strategy whereby you buy a put option with the expectation that the price of the stock will drop beyond the strike price before expiry.

These are very easy to set up since it's just a single option order.

Buy 1 ATM Put

Short Call Option

It's also known as Naked Call. A trader is expecting a steady or falling stock price during the life of the option.

These are very easy to set up since it's just a single option order.

Sell 1 OTM Call

15. Swing Trading

Swing trading refers to a trading style or method where traders seek to sell at potentially pivotal highs, and then reverse and buy at significant lows.

Means,

Buy at low and sell at high.

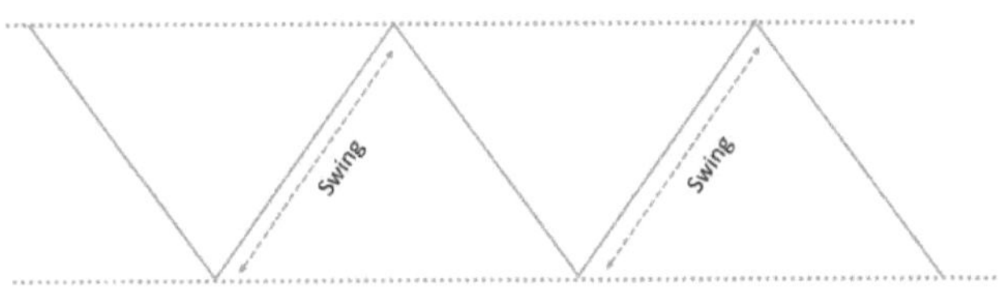

Fig. 27. Swings made by stock.

Strategy and Execution Rule for Swing Trading:

- Select stock with strong Fundamentals.

- Use Pivot Points(Support and Resistance) with a 1-day time frame.

- Sell when the stock closes above the resistance level and makes a false breakout.

- Buy at support levels.

- The target of stock can be 5-10% for 10-15 days.

- Stop-loss according to support and resistance levels.

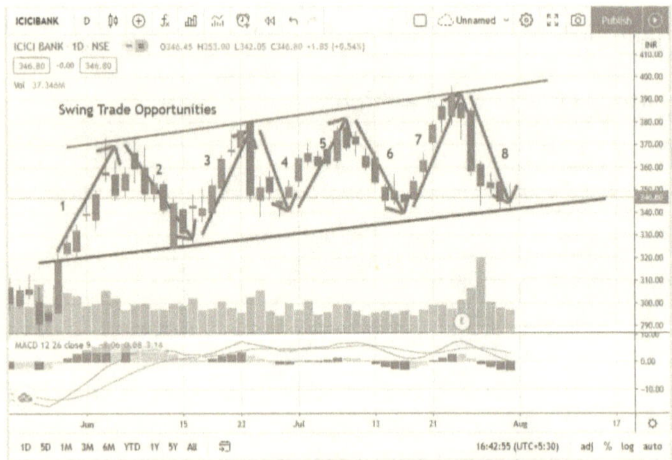

Fig. 28. ICICI Bank stock chart on a 1-day time frame. (Image Source and Credit: www.tradingview.com).

As we can see in the above fig. ICICI Bank gave us good swing trading opportunities. Stock trading in-between Resistance and Support levels give us good swing trades. ICICI Bank made good 8 swings and we can expect to bounce back from the support level and get the 9th swing for trading.

Fig. 29. Heromotoco stock chart on a 1-day time frame.(Image Source and Credit: www.tradingview.com).

Channel patterns can be considered to take swing trades. We can exit from our positions when we see channel breakout and can take breakout positions for another opportunity of trade.

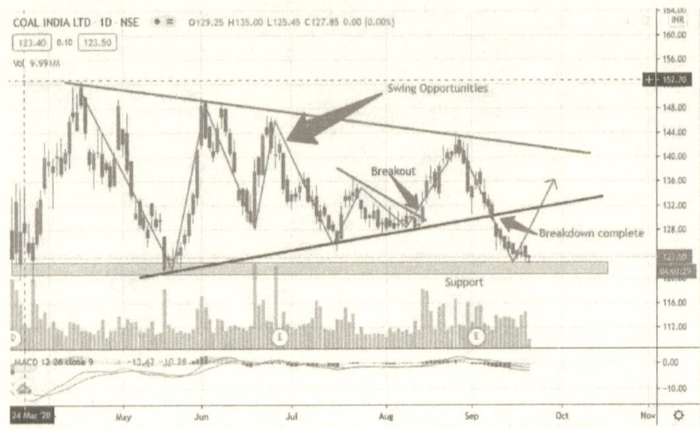

Fig. 30. Coal India stock chart on a 1-day time frame.
(Image Source and Credit: www.tradingview.com).

As we can see we had good opportunities for Swing Trades as well as Trend line Breakout and Breakdown trades opportunities in Fig.30 Coal India.

16. Scalping method for Intraday Trading

What is Scalping?

Scalping is a trading style specializing in taking profits on small price changes.

It requires a trader to have a strict exit strategy because one large loss could estimate the many small gains the trader has worked to obtain.

Constant attention is needed.

The only disciplined trader will succeed.

Why Bank Nifty Scalping?

- Bank Nifty is always a liquid instrument.

- Best volatile instrument available in the Indian stock market which is suitable for scalping.

- You can make a profit in any direction (up or down).

- Gives good returns on our capital (even 100% also).

- We can do many trades in a single day.

- Don't want to research a lot.

- Zero overnight position risk

- We can start with small capital

Strategy:

We use this strategy in Bank Nifty when the market is volatile and we want to catch the rally or big moves.

It requires less capital and also it has less risk.

For this strategy, we will select the Option call or put (CE/PE) not by STRIKE RATE but by selecting the premium.

Will select strike price with a premium range would be 30 to 120.

Now after selecting the strike price we need entry and exit points. Also, we need to select the call option when we are expecting Bank Nifty to move up and will select the Put option when we are expecting Bank Nifty to go down.

We require a Time Frame of 3Min and will watch the Call or Put options strike price chart to enter, not the Bank Nifty chart.

Will need to have a Three Candle pattern (1 Bearish and 2 Bullish candles) to get our criteria of entry.

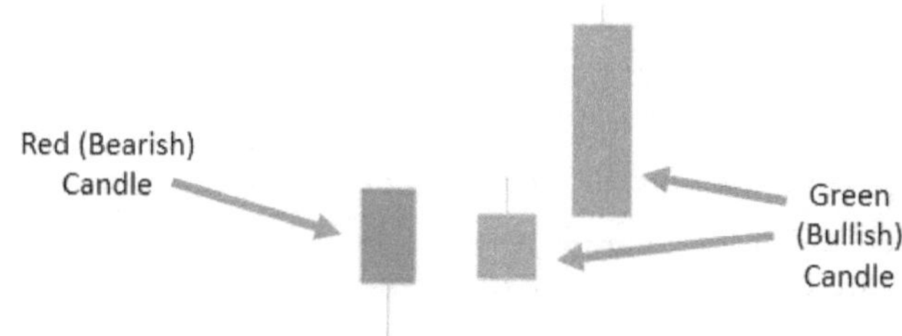

Fig. 31. Candle pattern.

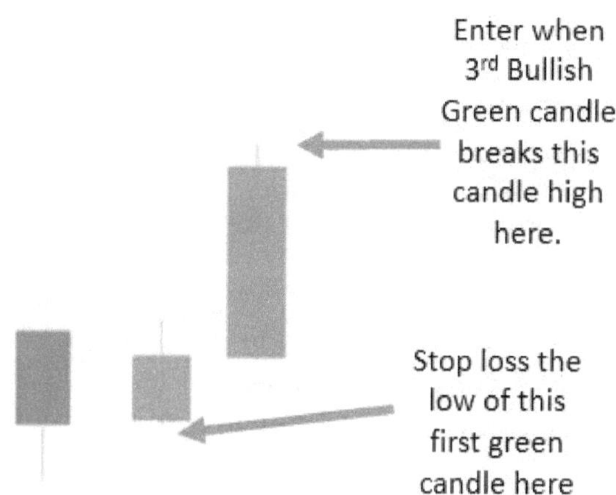

Fig. 32. Candle pattern.

Now we got our entry and stop loss. The target we can keep of 1:2 risk-reward ratio as of our stop loss. Suppose if our stop loss is 20 points then our first target will be 40 points. Will take 2 lots of multiple of 2 lots in this strategy and will book only 50% of quantities at the first target and keep trailing our stop loss so we can take more advantage of the rally. The second target we might get 1:5 or 1:10 also.

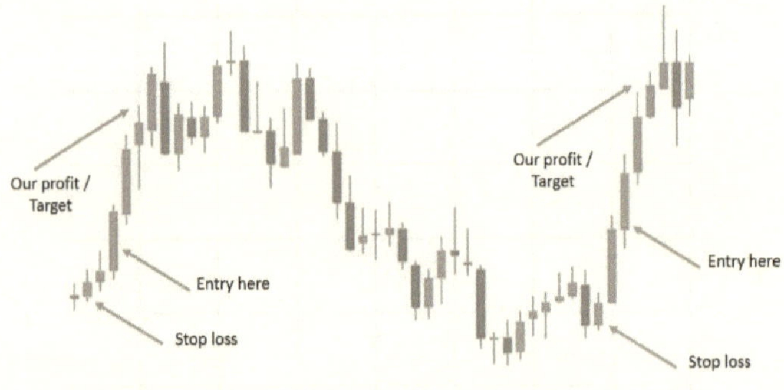

Fig. 33. Candle pattern chart of Call Option.

In the above fig, we can see two good opportunities and two good pattern formations to enter the trade and get profits. We can get those rallies and make a profit with proper entry and exit in the options trading.

17. Super Futures Strategy

This strategy can be used in Bank Nifty Futures for only Intraday Trading.

Strategy steps:

You need to have 15 minutes bar chart.

Follow the first 15 minutes bar in the chart.

Mark High and Low of that bar.

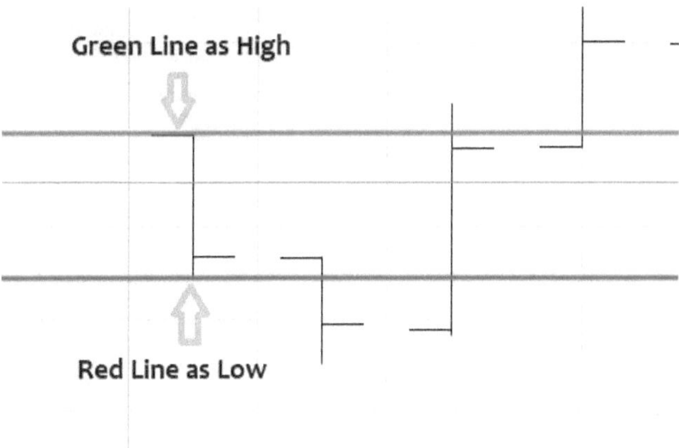

Fig. 34. Bar Chart of Bank Nifty on 15 minutes time frame.

4. Now the second bar candle will break either high or low of the first bar candle.

5. You have to take trade only if it breaks either high or low of the first candle.

6. Let's take an example, as shown in the above image if the second candle breaks the low of the first candle then will take a buy call. (Reversal Strategy)

7. Now, when the third candle breaks the high of the second candle, take entry at that point and trade in the call option. Put stop loss as shown in the image.

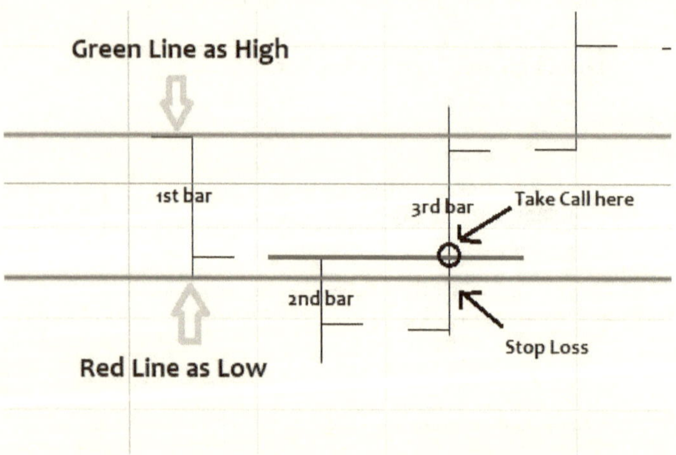

Fig. 35. Bar Chart of Bank Nifty on 15 minutes time frame.

8. Stop-loss is at the low of the first candle. Now when the next bar touches the high of the first candle, modify stop-loss, and put stop loss at a cost-to-cost point. i.e. stop loss where you took the entry.

9. So now you don't have any loss when the stop loss hits i.e. Zero Risk :)

Fig. 36. Bar Chart of Bank Nifty on 15 minutes time frame.

10. Lot Size of Nifty is 75. If you get 100 points in that trade you would earn 100*75 = 7500 /- profit in a single lot :)

Even if in some cases the stop loss hits in next or another day then you don't have to worry as that stop loss is very less and profit is so much if stop loss doesn't get hit. You could cover your stop loss of a full week in a single trade.

Try this strategy and work on it. As it doesn't need much research as you are a beginner. For a few days try this strategy and later on when you get enough time or you want to do full-time trading then you can try some more analytical strategies.

18. Simple Strategy

One of the simplest intraday trading strategies is:

Open = High

If the stock's opening candle, open and high are the same, wait for the first candle to close and if the next candle opens below the closing of the first candle SELL the stock with the first candle high as the STOP LOSS.

Draw a 14-period moving average on the chart, as time moves on keep this line as a trailing stop loss, book profits if the candle closes above the average moving line and the next candle opens higher than the previous candle.

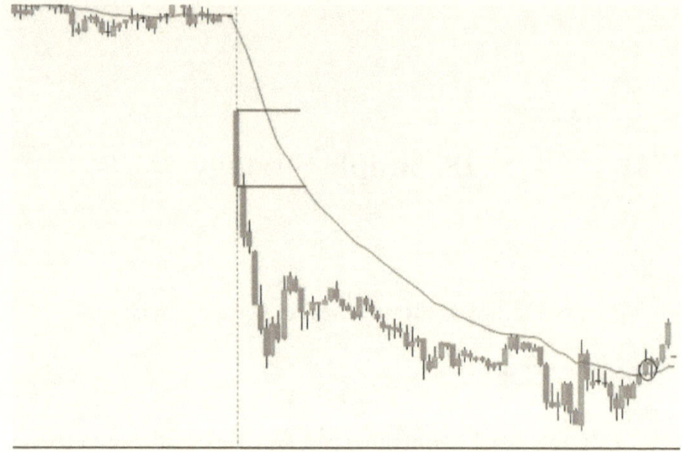

Fig. 37. Candle Chart of stock ((Image Source: Google)

Enter in the second candle and book profit at the circled candle.

Open = Low

If the stock's opening candle, open and low are the same, wait for the first candle to close, and if the next candle opens above the high the first candle BUY the stock with the first candle low as the STOP LOSS.

Draw a 14-period moving average on the chart, as time moves on keep this line as a trailing stop loss, book profits if the candle closes below the average moving line and the next candle opens lower than the previous candle.

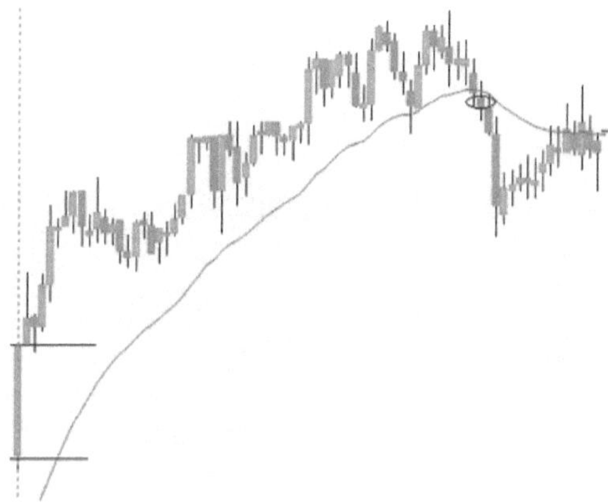

Fig. 38. Candle Chart of stock (Image Source: Google).

Enter in the second candle and book profit in the circled candle.

Note: Not all open=high and open=low will follow this copybook style. If it reverses we need to follow the rule and should not average the losing trades, just exit the trade as the defined rules.

19. Process to Master the Strategy

There is always a process to become a master in anything and we won't find any shortcuts.

1. Selecting a Market (Stock or Index (Nifty or Bank Nifty)):

As a beginner, one should either choose stock or index to trade. One should go all at a time. Identify your best resource to make money. It's stocks or Index.

2. Selecting a Time Frame (9.15 – 10.30, 10.30 – 12.30, 12.30 to 2.00, 2-3.30):

Indian Market has a pre-open time at 9.00 am and the market will get settled at 9.07 am. In the first session, from 9.15 to 10.30 am we can expect good volatility. Stock can open flat, gap up, or gap down. If we have good pre-open analysis skills then we can take the trade as soon as the market starts at 9.15 am.

Till 10.30 will have good data with us to analyze. At around 12.30 European market starts and Indian markets can react to those markets and trade accordingly. In the last session from 2.00 to 3.30 pm, we can see intraday traders squaring off their positions or new buyers buying or creating positions to carry forward. In all this period we need to identify our best time so we can trade accordingly. The market is different every other day and it doesn't need to work as explained. But it's in general thing and we need to understand this. In the full day, we can get good trade opportunities anytime and at any juncture, but we need a setup.

3. Selecting a Trading Style (Swing/Positional, Scalping, Intraday, Aggressive trading)

4. Defining Entry points

5. Defining Exit points

6. Evaluating your trading strategy

7. Improving your trading strategy

When we are trading in Index like Nifty and Bank Nifty then we should also track high weightage stocks in the Index. Nifty consists of 50 stocks and Bank Nifty consists of 8 bank stocks. In Bank Nifty top 5 weightage stocks own 65-70% of total weightage and so their movement will impact more on Bank Nifty like Kotak Bank, ICICI Bank, HDFC Bank, Axis, and SBI Bank.

When we are talking about learning the art of trading and technical analysis and strategies. We can't miss things called Indicators.

Right?

20. Trading with Indicators

A Technical Indicator is a series of data points that are derived by applying a formula to the price data.

The indicator is made up of Price. A formula is applied to price and we get indicators.

But the price is moved by NEWS.

Since indicator moves on price, many indicators run late and their accuracy is not 100%.

There are two categories as Leading Indicators and Lagging Indicators. And according to my experience, I can say that Lagging indicators are more accurate than leading indicators.

Moving Average

Moving Average is a tool used by a technical analyst that smooth's out price data by creating a constantly updated average price. The average price is taken over a specific period, like 50 days, 200 days.

One can trade on a single moving average and for a good result, one can combine 2 or 3 moving average indicators and trade on the crossover of those moving averages.

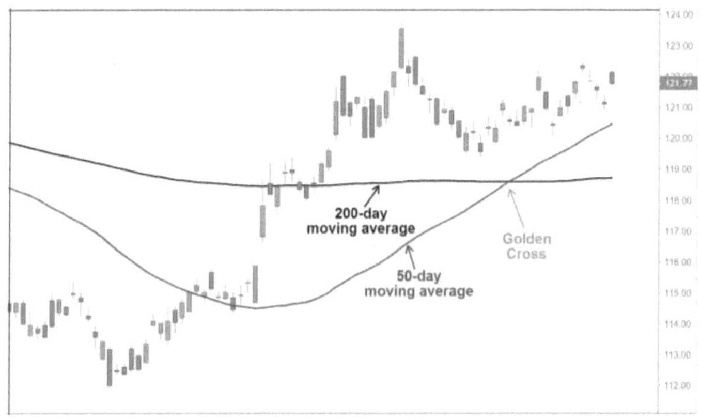

Fig. 40. Moving Average Indicator. (Image Source: Google)

As we can see above fig.40 a good golden cross of 50-day moving average on a 200-day moving average and that cross can turn our good trade opportunity.

MACD

The Moving Average Convergence Divergence (MACD) is a technical indicator that simply measures the relationship of Exponential Moving Averages (EMA). The MACD displays a MACD line (blue), the signal line (red), and a histogram (green) - showing the difference between the MACD line and the signal line.

These MACD lines waver in and around the zero lines. This gives the MACD the characteristics of an oscillator giving overbought and oversold signals above and below the zero-line respectively.

The MACD measures momentum or trend strength by using the MACD line and zero lines as reference points:

When the MACD line crosses ABOVE the zero lines, this signals an UPTREND

When the MACD line crosses BELOW the zero lines, this signals a DOWNTREND

Also, the MACD signals buy or sell orders which are given when the two MACD lines cross over as outlined below:

When the MACD line crosses ABOVE the signal line, traders use this as a BUY indication

When the MACD line crosses BELOW the signal line, traders use this as a SELL indication

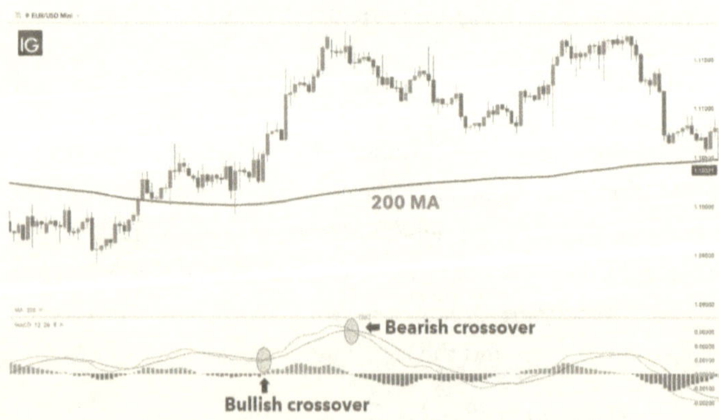

Fig. 41. MACD Indicator. (Image Source: Google)

Super Trend

Super Trend being a trending indicator works beautifully in trending markets (both uptrends and downtrends). The buy-sell signal can easily be identified when the indicator flips over the closing price. A buy signal is generated when the Super Trend closes below the price and the color changes to green. On the other hand, a sell signal is made when the Super Trend closes above the price and the color of Super Trend turns red.

There's no technical indicator that can be 100% accurate and so is Super Trend also. It also generates false signals in the sideways market, though it gives lesser false signals as compared to other indicators. So you can combine Super Trend with other indicators to get better trading signals.

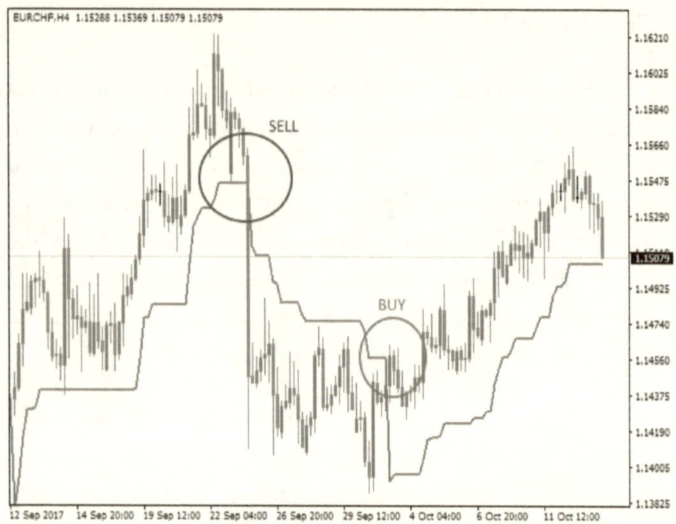

Fig. 42. Super Trend Indicator. (Image Source: Google)

Bollinger Band

Bollinger Bands, a technical indicator developed by John Bollinger, are used to measure a market's volatility and identify "overbought" or "oversold" conditions.

This little tool tells us whether the market is quiet or whether the market is LOUD!

When the market is quiet, the bands contract and when the market is LOUD, the bands expand.

It has the Middle line as a 20-day moving average, lower and upper bands. It generally indicates the volatility of the stock by a narrow or wider range of the bands.

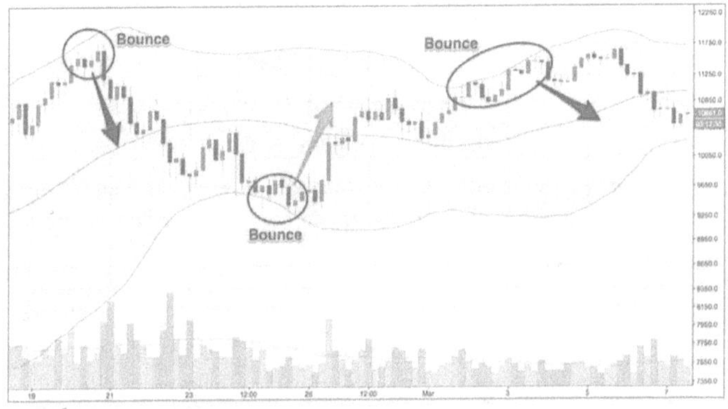

Fig. 43. Bollinger Band Indicator. (Image Source: Google)

Strategy on Bollinger Band:

An important point is 95% of the price is trading in Range. So will target a 5% area where will see exceptional high volatility.

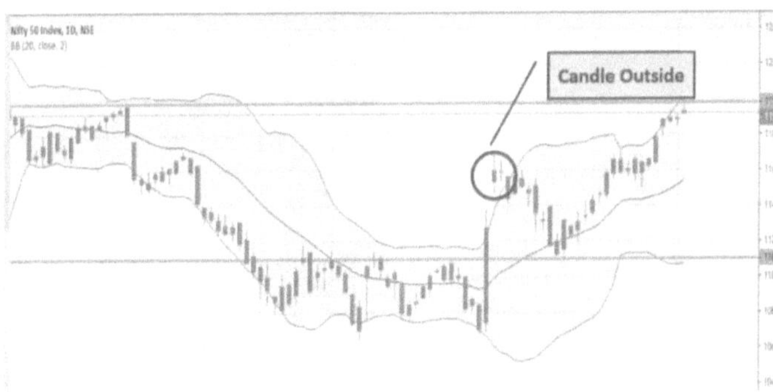

Fig. 43. Bollinger Band Indicator(Image Source: Google)

As seen in the above fig. Will target the candle which is trading outside the Bollinger Band. If the candle is trading outside the upper band then we can take a trade on the next candle which breaks the low of the first candle and our target can be the middle line of the Bollinger Band. Similarly, if a candle is trading outside the lower band then we can take a trade on the next candle which breaks the high of the first candle and our target can be the middle line of the   Bollinger Band Indicator.

Best setup:

For better confirmation and more accuracy, we can use multiple indicators and get double confirmations.

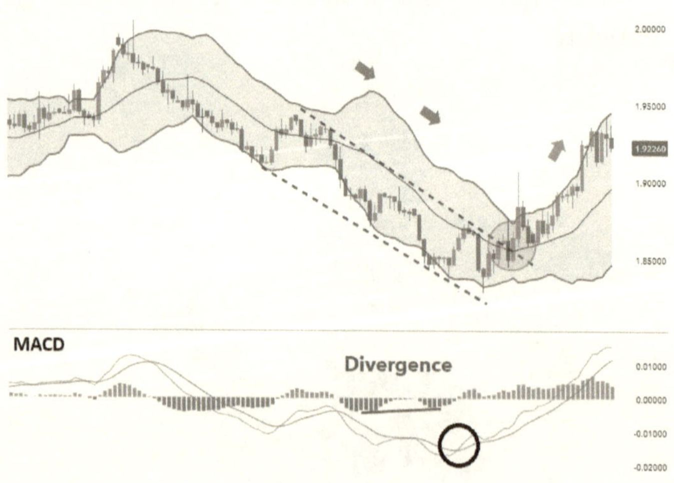

Fig. 44. Indicators. (Image Source: Google)

As seen in the above fig.44. We can see Trend line Breakout, MACD indication, Bollinger Band middle line bounce, and also Super trend buy signal. Such setups and more customized setups can be used by combining more than 2 indicators.

21. Characteristics of a Good Trader

To be a good trader one needs to have strong learning abilities. One should be able to control their emotions and should accept what the market gives us back. The acceptance and Never Give Up theory helps much to be a good trader.

Learn. Practice. Repeat!

One should have the capabilities of an eagle. I mean to say one shouldn't be a bull or bear of the market. A good trader is an Eagle.

Fig. 45. Eagle. (Image Source: Google)

Eagle waits long for their opportunities and grabs that perfectly whenever they see those opportunities. The skills to check, when you get that opportunity and when to attack play a big role. i.e. when to trade and when not to trade. When to take entry and when to exit from the trade. These skills make a trader a very good trader in the longer run.

Also,

Cobra, when they want to attack their spitting is spot on. They attack straight and perfect in the human eye.

Fig. 46. Cobra Snake. (Source: Google)

Even when a person moves, even when their wind flowing, even when the snake's position is not perfect. Snakes adjust well and know when to attack. They will check and calculate all the important and required things and will attack with perfect aim to the human eye.

These skills are perfect to analyze how one can aim their targets and find good opportunities in the market.

Executed orders (34)   Q Search   View Reports   Download

Time	Type	Instrument	Product	Qty.	Avg. price	Status
15:01:18	SELL	BANKNIFTY 4ᵗʰ JUN 20500 PE NFO	NRML	400 / 400	108.85	COMPLETE
15:00:51	BUY	BANKNIFTY 4ᵗʰ JUN 20500 PE NFO	NRML	400 / 400	104.46	COMPLETE
15:00:02	SELL	BANKNIFTY 4ᵗʰ JUN 21000 PE NFO	NRML	200 / 200	231.33	COMPLETE
14:59:50	BUY	BANKNIFTY 4ᵗʰ JUN 21000 PE NFO	NRML	200 / 200	223.89	COMPLETE
14:36:35	SELL	BANKNIFTY 4ᵗʰ JUN 22000 CE NFO	NRML	200 / 200	146.09	COMPLETE
14:36:16	BUY	BANKNIFTY 4ᵗʰ JUN 22000 CE NFO	NRML	200 / 200	143.78	COMPLETE
14:35:43	SELL	BANKNIFTY 4ᵗʰ JUN 22000 CE NFO	NRML	200 / 200	133.27	COMPLETE
14:35:12	BUY	BANKNIFTY 4ᵗʰ JUN 22000 CE NFO	NRML	200 / 200	131.91	COMPLETE
14:33:13	SELL	BANKNIFTY 4ᵗʰ JUN 21500 CE NFO	MIS	160 / 160	305.83	COMPLETE
14:32:49	BUY	BANKNIFTY 4ᵗʰ JUN 21500 CE NFO	MIS	160 / 160	296.66	COMPLETE
13:57:40	SELL	BANKNIFTY 4ᵗʰ JUN 21500 CE NFO	MIS	180 / 180	253.43	COMPLETE
13:57:35	BUY	BANKNIFTY 4ᵗʰ JUN 21500 CE NFO	MIS	180 / 180	249.83	COMPLETE

Fig. 47. Bank Nifty Trades (Image Source: www.zerodha.com)

All trades taken above are perfect examples of Scalping and perfect entry and exits. We can achieve these qualities with hard practice and learning things every day.

22. Building Professional Trading Mindset

Position Sizing plays an important role in building a professional trading mindset. Taking big quantities and seeing a few points' loss, your mind will get affected so always take small quantities first and gain confidence.

We need to keep our subconscious mind normal so will not miss good opportunities. Else will say, "That was really good trade and I would have taken". Don't get addicted to FOMO (Fear of Missing Out) things.

Plan and execute well with a professional mindset.

Now I will share two cases so you can choose one whichever you feel is better for you.

Case 1: Rahul trades with big quantities and aims for bigger profits at the initial stage. After a few trading sessions, the result was,

15k + 20k − 30k + 25k − 20k + 15k = 25k

Overall he made 25000 and lost most of his confidence when he was having that big 30000 and 20000 losses. Also, it used to have stress and tensions with losses and excitements with profits. He finally faced problems of anxiety and couldn't continue for a long time in the Share Market.

Case 2: Meena trades with small quantities and aims for smaller profits at the initial stage.

5k + 3k – 3k + 12k – 2k + 5k = 20k

Overall she made 20000 and gained some confidence and didn't fear much. She improved and maintained a good mindset and profit. Small profits and losses didn't make her get emotional with fear and greed things and so she stayed in the Market for a longer time.

Now when we compare both cases than they made some similar profits with little difference but important is one gained good confidence and the other lost the confidence. One traded with emotions and the other traded with a disciplined mindset. One stayed a long time in the market and the other couldn't stay in the market for a longer time.

What're the Rules to follow to stay in the market for a longer time?

Rules:

- When we are having continuous 3 days losses then don't trade for the next 3 trading days. Go back to study mode, refresh your mind.

- When your total loss for the month becomes 10% then stop trading for the entire month (Know when to take a break).

- If you're at a loss of 10% then don't infuse further capital for the month.

- If you are profitable take out your profits, keep the same capital again.

- Try to develop confidence first and then aim for bigger profits.

- Control your environment and deal with stress and emotions (Fear and Greed).

- Maintaining a trade journal (reports) is compulsory because trading is business, not a game.

Trading Psychology is very important when we need to stay in the share market for a longer time. Strategies and money management are crucial but a Good mindset and trading psychology play a big role in getting successful in the Share Market.

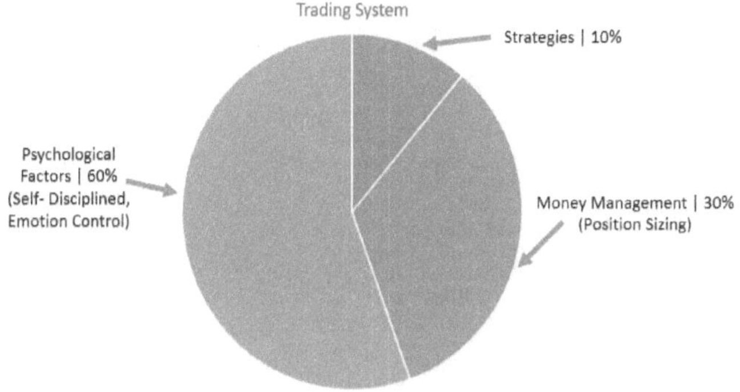

Fig. 49. Trading System.

As we can see in the above graph, strategies need only 10%, and psychological factors need a good 60% of what we called a successful trading system.

One needs trading experience to get that good trading psychological factor. Just reading or getting training sessions won't help much, but with the self-trading experience, we can learn a lot. Quick decision-making skills, emotion control skills, maintaining well-disciplined are all important things that we need to learn with getting some trading experience alongside.

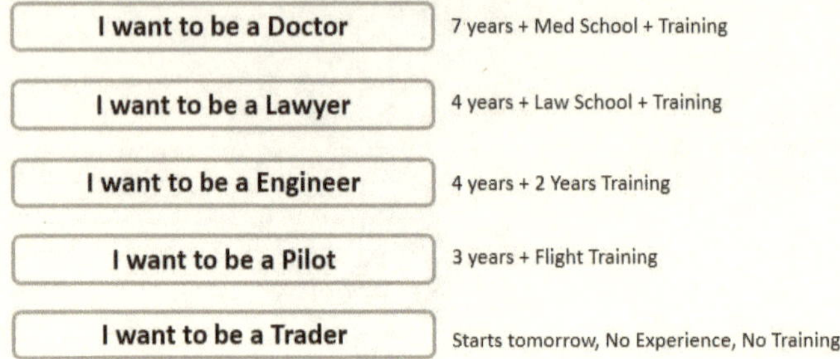

Fig. 50. Career period.

Trade like you have only one trade to take in whole one month. Trade with preparations and setups. Don't take trade just because you hope or feel to take a trade.

Profit and Losses are part of trading and we should challenge ourselves to maintain the starting capital at the end of the month.

Gaining positivity is important so take small profits. Play like you're playing a Test match and you need to play the full 5 days. Don't lose a wicket on the first day and first session.

Markets aren't going anywhere. We are here for at least 30 years. But if you fail to make your foundation robust, what is the guarantee that you will leave with your capital.

Never fight with the market. Respect the profession. Respect the market. Don't take revenge trades. Loss or Profit, respect the market and the market will respect us one day for sure.

Epilogue

Thank You

I wish you all the success ahead in your journey.

I fear not the man who has practiced 10,000 kicks once, but I fear the man who has practiced one kick 10,000 times.

– Bruce Lee

Practice 3-4 strategies again and again, and try to improve them according to your trading setup and trading mindset. I am confident that the Never Give Up theory and learning practices will make you an independent trader for sure.

"Take up one idea. Make that one idea your life; dream of it; think of it; live on that idea. Let the brain, the body, muscles, nerves, every part of your body be full of that idea, and just leave every other idea alone. This is the way to success, and this is the way great spiritual giants are produced."

–   Swami Vivekananda

To live a dream life we don't need to search for shortcuts. We need to be disciplined and smart. No virus can stop us from chasing our dreams!

Thank You

Will surely appreciate your valuable feedbacks.

WhatsApp – 7972172484

Email id – mukesh.bconsultant@gmail.com

Website – www.mukeshjangid.in

Disclaimer: These are just my personal views and are shared only for educational purposes. One can take advice from his/her financial advisor for making any investments in the Share Market or any business. Images Credits to www.google.com, www.tradingview.com, and www.zerodha.com.

Stay tuned for the next volume of the book!